AF540626

ESSAYS ON SCHOOL ISSUES

ESSAYS ON SCHOOL ISSUES

By

Dr. Marlow Ediger
Emeritus Professor of Education
Truman State University
201 West 22nd Street
North Newton KS 67117
United States of America
&

Dr. Digumarti Bhaskara Rao
M.Sc., M.A., M.A., M.Ed., Ph.D.
Principal & Professor
R.V.R. College of Education
D-43 (277) S.V.N. Colony
Guntur - 522 006 (India)
&
Member of Board of Studies in Education
Acharya Nagarjuna University
Nagarjuna Nagar - 522 510 (India)

DISCOVERY PUBLISHING HOUSE PVT. LTD.
NEW DELHI-110 002

Published by:
Tilak Wasan

DISCOVERY PUBLISHING HOUSE PVT. LTD.
4383/4B, Ansari Road, Darya Ganj
New Delhi-110 002 (India)
Phone : +91-11-23279245, 43596064-65
Fax : +91-11-23253475
E-mail : parul.wasan@gmail.com
discoverypublishinghouse@gmail.com
web : www.discoverypublishinggroup.com

***First Edition:* 2013**

ISBN: 978-93-5056-264-2

Essays on School Issues

Printed at:
Dynamic Printers
Delhi

Dedicated to
the Affectionate Statesman

DR. RAYAPATI SRINIVAS
Member of Legislative Council
Andhra Pradesh

Preface

School is an institution designed for the teaching of students under the direction of teachers. School expectations have proven to be challenging and overwhelming for students. It can be tough learning that the student is having difficulties and other issues in school, whether they're social, educational, or behavioural. It can also be very difficult to take the first steps in helping the student address the underlying issues that are causing those difficulties. But as a responsible and caring one, it's the teacher's job to help the students get past their issues at school and make it a place for effective learning.

Several issues concerned to curriculum, school and teacher are discussed in this book. This book will be of great use to the teachers and administrators at school.

Digumarti Bhaskara Rao

Contents

Locus of Control and the Pupil in the School Setting

Locus of control rests upon the theory that pupils take risks in achievement if they believe that success is forthcoming. The objective has to be worthwhile in attainment with the belief that effort might produce the end goal. These pupils feel inwardly that motivation toward the objective or goal will be productive. Control resides within the self. Toward the other end of the continuum, a pupil might believe that it is extrinsic influences which make for success in goal attainment. Thus, parents, the teacher, the material used in study and luck, amongst other factors, produce the end results. There are also in between positions in the continuum, between intrinsic *versus* extrinsic factors (Balaji, 2010).

Who Is In Control?

Control might then reside inside or outside the influence of the human being, according to the opposing positions or points of view. This debate may also involve, in degrees, heredity as compared to the environment in ascertaining occurrences. With heredity, a teacher, for example, is a born teacher, largely possessing the knowledge, skills and attitudes, necessary for good teaching. Most would not go to this extreme. They tend to feel that capable teachers, in degrees, are also developed through a plethora of educational opportunities. Those who believe strongly that good teaching capabilities are developed, not inborn, believe that environmental forces tend to prevail. It is then learned behaviour and is the position taken by many anthropologists and sociologists.

There are differences, however, in locus of control psychologists as compared to the heredity *versus* the environment advocates. Locus of control, internal *versus* external, analyze/separate the two influences, in terms of:

- decision making. Who decides what to do in a given point of time or situation, is it the individual or fate?
- selected factors, positive or negative, make choices go either way. Behaviour may well be learned to be optimistic or pessimistic for guiding one's thought process.
- social conditions influence the choices made, whether they be affluent or poverty stricken.
- economic factors, such as high employment *versus* recession/depression.
- many job opportunities as compared to facing difficulties in securing a vocation of choice, for university graduates, in particular (see Ediger 2011).

In 1966, Julian Rotter originally stated the following pertaining to locus of control: 'Internal control' is the term used to describe the belief that future outcomes reside primarily in oneself, while 'external control' refers to the expectancy that controls is outside oneself, either in the hands of powerful or other people or due to fate/chance (as quoted in Balaji, p. 8).

Human expectations are involved in terms of who is in control of happenings. Thus, those with inward motivation thinking emphasize the following:

- teachers need to get pupils enthusiastic to learn with stimulating lessons and units of study. A few pupils possess this motivation to begin with;

- encourage learners to achieve aids motivation;
- providing readiness experiences helps pupils to perceive connections with the new objectives of instruction;
- pupils being involved in sequencing their knowledge, skills, and attitudes assist to attain new learnings;
- advanced organizers used by the teacher aid pupils in building background information in order to understand the ensuing lesson (Ediger 2010).

Pupils who believe that the environment is friendly/unfriendly for achieving goals need to

- be guided to show that they can achieve with effort put forth;
- choose self selected studying material which is interesting with interests propelling attainment;
- receive assistance from teachers to choose materials of instruction, based on the pupils present attainment levels;
- experience success in ongoing learning activities which provide a basis for future endeavours;
- have adequate background information before having pursued a lesson/unit of study;
- review previous learnings to connect with the ensuing experiences;
- experience scaffolding to obtain more complex subject matter (See Walston, Walston, and DeVillus, 1978).

Conclusion

The question remains, yet is—does the locus of control reside within the individual or does luck—fate have an increased power? The following are observed when people believe more in the latter or environmental factors when making a statement of after a choice has been made:

- knocking on wood. Always carrying a miniature rabbit's foot, or other good luck charm, is further evidence to believe in luck for pursuing a correct path;
- crossing one's fingers;

- "buttoning one's coat right" for an interview in securing a position or job.

For those who believe in the locus of control being intrinsic, much effort, work, and quality reasoning aid in goal achievement. The teacher needs to consider where the locus of control resides within pupils in the classroom. Those who feel more closely in achieving a goal will more likely put forth needed effort in whatever the objective pertains to. There is a probability concept involved here (See Rotter.1989).

REFERENCES

Balaji, P. S. (2010), Impact of Locus of Control on Emotional Intelligence. Karaikudi, India: Alagappa University, India. *Ph.D. Thesis,* Education.

Ediger, Marlow (2011), "Mentoring in the Social Studies," *College Student Journal*, 45 (2), 233-237.

Ediger, Marlow, and D. Bhaskara Rao (2010), *Essays in Teaching Social Studies.* New Delhi, India: Discovery Publishing House.

Rotter, J.B. 1980, "Internal *Versus* External of Reinforcement. *A Case History of a Variable, American Psychologist*, 45, 489-493

Wallston, K.A., Wallston, B.S., and R. Devillus (1978), Development of the Multi-Dimensional Health Locus of Control, *Health Education Demographics*, Volumes 6, 160-170.

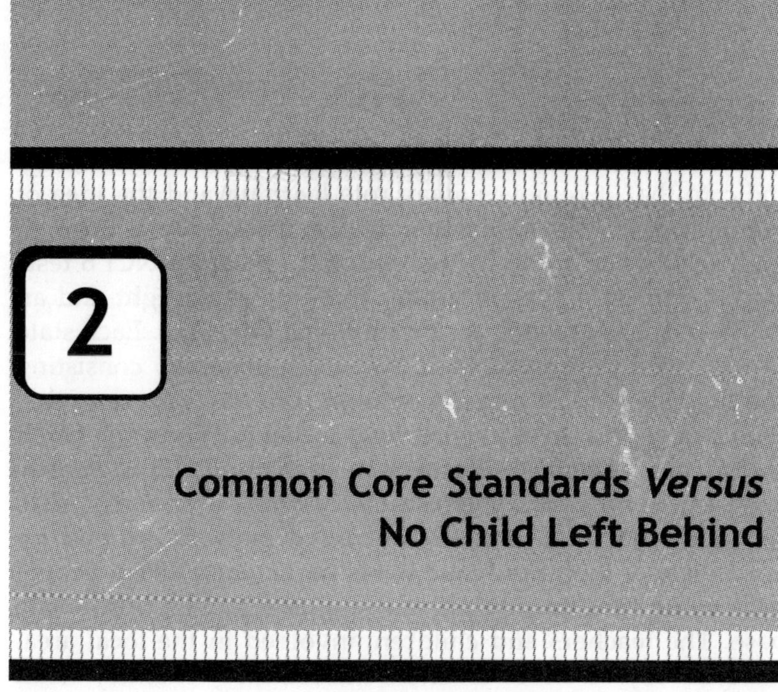

2

Common Core Standards *Versus* No Child Left Behind

Much is written and discussed pertaining to both the Common Core standards *versus* No Child Left Behind (NCLB). The common core has been adopted by most states in the union and was developed in answer to problems faced in NCLB. The common core objectives and tests are to be taken by all the pupils in the US whereas each state developed their own tests in NCLB, thus making comparisons in pupil achievement is impossible, among the different states since much depended upon the difficulty level of test items in each state's NCLB (See, Shea and Shanahan, 2011).

Making the Comparisons

The common core standards, unifier among all states in the union, has the same tests for all pupils in a particular grade level. They are written on the national level, whereas NCLB is developed on the level of each state. The common core has selected open ended test questions such as pupils writing an essay on a particular grade level. Others are multiple choice test items where there is one correct answer among the four options options in one question. Thus, the common core wishes to assess learners on creative endeavours also. They indicate that it removes away rote learning and the idea of memorization. The common core also tracks pupils through high school and up to higher education whereas NCLB tests pupils once in a year in grades three through eight and an exit test in high school, for promotional purposes. Each state in the union developed their own tests, generally consisting multiple choice test items. Common core advocates say that their test is on a level playing field for all pupils in the US. It is true that the same test is taken by each pupil within a grade level, but abilities and interests can and do differ much. Also, to have objectives and standardized tests developed by specialists in their academic fields particularly stress people determining the curriculum who are far removed from home base. The teachers and children, involved in the local area, have no say so here. Teachers immediately identify what pupils do not understand as well as misunderstandings inherent in the learning act. They may diagnose what learners need within each teaching and learning situation (Ediger and Rao, 2011). Amongst others, the teacher notices the following, (Ediger, 2003):

- Pupils, who are actively involved in learning. Learning experiences must be provided for each learner to participate actively.
- Pupils, who attach meaning to facts, concepts, and generalizations being pursued. A lack of understanding may need scaffolding for pupils to achieve.
- Pupils, who lack purpose in learning. Here, the teacher needs to explain reasons for pursuing a lesson or unit of study. Inductively, pupils also might be assisted to perceive purpose.
- Pupils, who need to gain proficiency in social intelligence (SI), and the ones who need help socially (not necessarily charismatic, behaviour).
- Pupils, who need assistance in emotional intelligence (El), see (Mohanty and Mohanty, 2011).

Helping pupils persevere is another quality dimension of learner behaviour which is not covered in the common core standards neither NCLB, and yet it is very salient. Those who do not give up but continue to strive until a project or activity is completed are certainly a valuable trait. When supervising university students, teachers, the writer noticed that how pupils with perceived lesser abilities put forth much energy in task completion and yet did well while having this trait. Pupils with higher abilities might as well be even more successful if they would strive in spite of difficulties. Even than, to make for higher attainment, these learners may be aided through scaffolding, either by the teacher or when working collaboratively with others. Perseverance is certainly a vital characteristic which assists pupils to be successful achievers (See Mendel, 2006). Additionally, intrinsic motivation needs encouragement in that pupil from inside for a desire to achieve, grow, and accomplish. Those not possessing inward motivation need guidance and direction whereby the teacher provides learning experiences which interest and encourage pupils.

Open-mindedness is an important personality aspect for pupils. Selected pupils are not receptive of innovative ideas. Their minds seemingly are closed, also, to the more traditional content. Wanting to learn is a salient personality characteristic which makes for growth, achievement, and progress in learning. Society needs individuals who are curious and enthusiastic to gain new, positive ideas. Where these types of individuals in achievement, have made for progress in the social arena (See Guccione, 2011). When pupils are in schools and classrooms, it is difficult to identify the ones who will contribute much to change for an improved and developed society. Pupils, for example, might learn more about change and new ideas with the following subject matter, amongst others, which might as well serve as a model to assist learners to be openminded and curious.

The writer grew up on a farm and in an era when draft horses with gang plows were used to till farm land. Harrows, too, to smoothen the plowed acres, pulled by draft horses were being phased out rapidly in the early 1930s. The rapid dawn of tractors, then came out, pulling the mower to cut hay, followed by a dump rake which raked the hay in small piles so a pitch fork could be used to load the hay onto a wagon. The hay was then pitched from the wagon into a large stack in a barn or shed, to prevent spoilage. This was used for winter feed for livestock on the farm. Subject matter, such as this, helps pupils to see that changes must be made in machines and inventions to meet human needs.

Presently, farm operations are conducted with machines and automation. Thus, the following are in evidence:

- tractors with air conditioned cabs freeing the operator from dust and extreme temperatures;
- hay balers, pulled by tractors, which pick up the cut hay from windrows, and baled. These bales may weigh 1100 pounds; the older model balers produced sixty pound bales which were either round (cylindrical) or square;
- the large, or small, hay bales are picked up with a front end loader on a tractor to haul them to where the cattle are located. The large bales may also be loaded on an eighteen wheeler to be sold and taken to a more distant feeding lot of livestock, where approximately 800 head of cattle are fed. The size of the feeding lot may be increasingly larger or smaller. The learner needs to benefit from these, as well as from other units of study, in securing relevant facts, concepts, and generalizations. Key structural ideas must be stressed in ongoing learning experiences, not the irrelevant and not the insignificant. Activities to achieve objectives must contain quality sequence with meaningful learnings. Classrooms must move from being teacher centred to being pupil centred (See Brown, 2003).

Also, a resource person with up to date illustrations should be invited into the classroom to talk about modern egg production facilities as well as for mass production of hogs. There are high costs involved to purchase/buy latest in equipment in farming. Pupils need to be guided to learn about change in other facts of society.

Innovations have made work easier as well as more productive with farm operations, here, used as an example. Manual labour in many situations has made work more efficient and enjoyable. In some situations, labour intensive work is still performed, for example, by migrant farm workers in hand picking strawberries as well as obtaining low wages in these kinds of dead end jobs.

Conclusion

The writer has attempted to point out how standardized tests may determine a limited curriculum by omitting major leanings to be acquired by pupils. There is a plethora of additional traits which needs development, other than those in the knowledge and cognitive domains. The creative mind brings on innovations which may benefit everyone in the social arena. Quality human relations make situations in school and society more enjoyable as well as assisting improved communication among individuals and groups. Progress in most of these areas may be observed by the classroom teacher without the use of standardized tests. Assistance must be provided pupils when needed, such as emphasizing objectives in collaborative endeavours in the classroom setting.

REFERENCES

Brown, David (2003), "Learner Centred Conditions that Ensure Student Success in Learning," *Education*, 124 (1), 99-104.

Ediger, Marlow, and D. Bhaskara Rao (2011), *Essays on Teaching and Learning*. New Delhi, India: Discovery Publishing House.

Ediger, Marlow (2003), 'Teacher Involvement to Evaluate Achievement,' *Education*, 124 (1),137-142.

Guccione, Lindsey (2011), Integrating Literacy and and Inquiry for English Language Learners," *The Reading Teacher*, 64 (8), 567-577.

Mendel, Scott (2006), "What New Teachers Really Need," *Educational Leadership*, 63 (6), 66-71.

Mohanty, Mamita and Jitandra Mohandy (2011),"Promoting Wellness Among School Children," *Edutracks*, 10 (11), 11-12.

Shea, Lauren, and Therese Shanahan, (2011), "Methods and Strategies," *Science and Children* 49(3), 62-66.

3

Disagreements with Selected Educational Goals

Why all the emphasis rests upon what selected educators and policy makers recommend? There are salient ideas in education which are advocated continuously. It almost sounds like a stuck record. There needs to be an adequate debate and discussion among public school personnel, teachers, university professors, educational philosophers and psychologists to agree upon what should be emphasized in the curriculum. Educators must have their voices expressed in a rational discussion, not like some town meetings we have heard on television during the presidential campaign. Neither should these meetings emphasize opinions as are given in a TV newscast whereby those with opposite beliefs shout at each other, refusing to hear what the opposition says. Nothing is accomplished with rudeness, intimidation, making damaging remarks, and setting the stage for dissension. Rather, civility should be prevailed where quality listening occurs among knowledgeable people. Quality background information should be at the finger tips of participants. The moderator in debates needs to be as unbiased as possible and enforce established rules. He/she must be a good listener and contribute expertise, he/she should not make dogmatic statements which cannot be substantiated with critical remarks. A shouting match does not accomplish anything but hostility and anger. Merely trying to confuse the participants by making remarks other participants with "holier than thou" is defeating and not rational/moral. Rather, carefully construed ideas based on an adequate knowledge, as well as theory, should prevail.

Participants must be informed about the issues being discussed. Decisions need to be based on the psychology of learning and how it affects pupils in teaching and learning situations, not on haughtiness, aloofness and the profit motive. Dogmatic thinking must be avoided.

Setting Standards

When listening to the policy makers, one thinks is that education consists of standards set in advance for pupil achievement. The standards movement stresses that the basics identified by policy makers must be achieved by all pupils. It eliminate the fact that learners differ from each other in a multiplicity of ways such as interest, motivation, purpose, and abilities. Why all the emphasis is placed upon standards? Could it be that regardless of standards of achievement by pupils, it is not adequate and needs to be lambasted by higher ups who are divorced from teaching? What justification is there for pupils acquiring the knowledge and skills in these standards? It appears that pupils and teachers thinking does not matter in selecting objectives. One wonders what correlation would there be between pupils doing well on the tests and future success at the work place or happiness in life.

In few cases/on very few occassions, standards, such as No Child Left Behind (NCLB) represents punishment if pupils do not attain what is deemed necessary, such as not being promoted from one grade level to the next. If pupils fail, the self concept goes downhill. It may be justified to have some kind of criteria to govern "what should be in education," but these need to be:

- voluntary to notice how well pupils 'measure up' to selected criteria
- used as one standard, among others, in promotion of pupils
- stressed as objectives for pupils to achieve with others, as determined by teachers and pupils, as well as school principals
- flexible so that meaningful learning opportunities can be chosen, involving pupil/teacher input
- written so that teaching to a test is not recommendable or possible.

Test results do not necessarily determine how well a student/pupil will do in life. Outside the formal education, individuals do not take tests to reveal how they can perform at a work place. It is the quality deeds and acts that matter. Testing is one method to ascertain how well a pupil is achieving, but other means are also available such as observations made by the teacher, pupil/teacher evaluation of the former's progress using recommended standards, portfolios, as well as using constructivism as a psychology of learning in the classroom. Then too, policy makers have a hangup of documentation of pupil achievement to track progress. Documentation, too frequently, means repetitious recording of test scores of pupils, over time. In contrast, voluntary test scores for each pupil might be recorded to notice progress of a pupil over previous tests taken. A single test to determine promotion places too much stress on the learner as well as the teacher. Any evaluation should answer the question, "Is the particular pupil achieving more gradually than previously?"

Quality Teaching and Learning

The standards movement seemingly does not take an account of an important part of curriculum development and that is learning opportunities for pupils. Learning opportunities should assist pupils to attain objectives of instruction, but not necessarily the ones chosen by policy makers. Objectives need to be flexible and open ended. Pupil input here is also salient. Who is to say that policy makers have the holy grail to ascertain these ends? Certainly, pupil interests and purposes also have merit. Adults would not like to have dictated what is to be read, studied, and pursued in terms of goals in life. Thus, pupil interests must be a valuable consideration in learning opportunities in the classroom. Pupils as well as adults do better in life if they can pursue what is of interest. Learning opportunities can be made interesting and teachers must keep the interest factor in mind when choosing which learning opportunities pupils have to pursue.

Pupil purpose, is also significant. Without purpose or reasons for learning, pupils achieve very little, generally. Building purpose for learning is time well spent in any lesson or unit of study. Thus, pupils need to perceive knowledge and skills as being relevant and having used in society. Perceiving the importance of what is being studied is vital. It is good if pupils can personally relate to content studied in the language arts, social studies, mathematics, and science. The scope needs to be broadened to include music, art, and physical education, rather than a narrow reading and mathematics emphasis as it is presently the case. Multiple intelligences theory indicates that there is more to life than just reading and calculating. Pupils have talents and abilities in other curriculum areas, also.

And also, meaning must be emphasized, in ongoing activities. Learning activities then must make sense. Merely covering pages in a textbook and learners not attaching meaning to vital facts, concepts, and generalizations encountered wastage of time and is costly in actual achievement. Rather, the following factors need consideration in teaching and learning:

- going from the known to the unknown
- perceiving sequence in learning
- relating content studied to the self, to others, as well as other vital ideas encountered.

When standards are set prior to instruction, are these important and relevant to learners involved in their achievement? If not the teacher must attempt to induce saliency within learners. The standards movement comes from human beings who in return write objectives for pupil attainment. They should not be looked upon as being absolutes, in and of themselves, but rather consist of broad guidelines which give leeway to interpretation. Thus, there is flexibility in teacher decision making to adapt these and other objectives to where pupils are presently achieving. They also may need adjusting to harmonize with the entire school curriculum. A rigid form of behaviour with its precise measurably stated objectives stresses a formal curriculum which tends to become factual in its leanings. Multiple choice test items appearing on high stakes testing have pupils zero in knowledge to determine the correct response of four distractors. There is no room then for quality critical and creative thinking. The correct answer must then be identified within multiple choice test items. With critical thought, pupils analyze the given matter before arriving at a conclusion. Then with creative thinking, the learner comes up with unique ideas which are original and novel. Behaviourism leaves little room for thinking of alternatives, other than what is presented in a multiple choice test. Life does not consist of choosing from four given alternatives in a test, in order to make every day decisions.

Charter Schools

Charter schools are growing rapidly in number. Originally, charters were set free of many governmental regulations in order to experiment with better teaching ideas than those exemplified in the public schools. They are funded as a part of the money which otherwise would go entirely to the public schools. There are a plethora of charter schools and this makes it, indeed, difficult to say how innovative they are. And, if exempt from standards which apply to the public schools, it is difficult to ascertain if pupils truly do better in these schools. There is a plethora of questions which needs to be answered pertaining to charters:

- Do public schools do less well when moneys are siphoned which go to charter schools?
- How can charters show effectiveness when they are freed from public school evaluations?
- Why all the clamour for implementation of charter schools?
- Why not improve present day public schools?
- How do they figure in with the turn around schools movement?

If selected governmental regulations are harmful to the public schools, why are these not done away with? Certainly, one does not want to implement what is harmful to pupils. How can comparisons then be made between charters and the public schools?

Closing the Gap in Achievement

Much is written about closing the gap in achievement between the dominant group and minorities. I gather this means, in my interpretation of the educational literature, to mean that the minority group must catch up and hold the dominant group to lower levels of progress. Each student needs to achieve as much as possible with high quality teachers, materials of instruction and supervisory aid. Time and time again, researches have shown that schools do more poorly in poverty areas. Poverty hinders pupils from experiencing the good life with excellent library books in their houses, visiting places of educational importance, taking vacations to nearby and remote areas, as well as different kinds of travel, among other possibilities. This indicates that much more must be done to eliminate/minimize poverty. The late President Lyndon Johnson was greatly concerned about the evils of poverty with his Great Society emphasis. The view that anything done to benefit the lower income person is 'socialist,' or 'communist' is absurd. Each family must have quality and safe housing, adequate and nutritious food, and proper clothing. This should be a human right and considered to be humane. One person should not own one or more mansions with twin indoor swimming pools containing different temperature readings of water and an eighteen hole golf course in a push area of the city/country, while selected others are homeless and hungry. Also, adequate health and dental care should be a right, not privilege, for everyone. These are salient for all pupils as well as adults to posses and do well in society.

How people are taxed by law will matter much in the amount of disposable income available to buy the good things in life. Laws whereby the upper income levels are given tax breaks as was done during the time a war is fought is not justifiable. Justifying these tax breaks on the basis of stimulating the economy is ridiculous. Fighting wars, too, should be discouraged, such as invading a nation due to false reports involving weapons of mass distraction. There is much which can be used to improve society if wars were not popular with selected groups of lay people. Fundamentalism is a cause for a plethora of wars and leads to extremism. Fighting wars is very expensive; there is much killing, wounding, maiming, and destruction of property. There can be bankruptcies of nations and demoralization as a result. Social programmes can thrive if the following exist:

- everyone pays taxes which are due to the different levels of government. Leona Helmsley's statement that only poor people pay taxes probably is true in too many cases. When cabinet positions were made to the recently elected president, the person designated Secretary of Health and Welfare had to step aside due to owing a hefty among of money to the federal government, around $150,000. How many others are there who owe money to the federal government?
- advertisements were taken off the air by companies offering their services to reduce taxes for individuals. It should definitely be made illegal to offer these 'services.' These commercial companies do not give examples of people who say that they are forced unjustly to pay a

certain amount of tax money. One couple in the TV ad state they owed $3 million dollars and the commercial company assisted them in paying less than one million dollars in federal income tax.

- the statement that "Social Security will go bankrupt, and we all know it, by the year 2015" is definitely untrue, especially if taxes were paid above the $102,000 level of income. Why not extend the level of taxation upward indefinitely? Then there would be less need for hysteria and people who have the income will not suffer for paying more into Social Security. The two tier society of the wealthy and the poor needs rethinking in terms of what it means for a democracy.
- eliminating badly written legislation and adding what is fair. CEOs of huge corporations and large companies who receive huge salaries such as twenty million dollars a year with bonuses and stock options, even if a business enterprise is failing are absurd and definitely unjustifiable.

Better laws need to be written and put into operation. Legislators need to be held accountable for unfortunate laws. Thus, one can bankrupt a corporation/company with huge salaries, excessive bonuses, and multiplicity of stock options and not commit a crime whereas in stealing a $5 package of meat, the involved person may be arrested, booked, and even imprisoned.

4

Curriculum Changes

Improving School Attendance

More needs to be done to improve pupil school attendance. This is a problem in many schools. Pupils lack sequence in learning due to the constant missing of classes by not coming to schools. Valuable lessons are omitted. New lessons and chapters lessons and their consequences are built upon previous learning experiences; failure to attend school creates omissions as well as lower achievement. There, of course, are justifiable reasons for not attending such as illness. But, very often, pupils miss school due to flimsy reasons such as taking care of the pet dog or cat. To encourage school attendance, the school environment needs to be free from dangers, including the following:

- harassment in its different forms.
- bullying situations.
- unkind, uncaring teachers and supervisors.
- racial prejudice and bias.
- rude attitude of students to each other.
- Teachers being less motivative and effective to the class therefore (Ediger, 2008).

Undoubtedly, learning becomes uneffective the entire classroom or school is having a negative atmosphere; pupils might wish to stay away from school when unpleasant settings occur. Even, a home setting which is uncaring, hostile, as well as a neighbourhood fraught with dangers, etc. Poverty is a major item which causes failture, where don't encourage pupils to stay there learners suffer from inadequate food, clothing, medical care, and shelter. In winter, one wishes to warm one self with heat or might want to have meat to keep onself up. It is no secret that suburban schools where family income is high, students learn and achieve at a much higher rate than in lower income urban schools (See Kindervater, 2010).

Students should have a safe environment in doing up & down to school. A lot of pupils are afraid of going to school, as well as what happens during school time, andvit causes lack as a result of attendance.

Improving School Attendance

There is so much that teachers can do in lesson and unit planning which, in its implementation can improve learner attendance. The writer has/we have noticed the area of interest of students while supervising universities. The writer has noticed the interest factor in pupil progress. The interest factor permeates excitement in learning. There are planned lessons which fascinate children and their attention is focussed upon what is being presented. These children are then interested in what transpires, not on boredom, nor misbehaviour. Thus, for example, when children watch tadpoles moving around in a gallon glass container, filled with pond water, their wholehearted fascination with these acts is remarkable. Here, they have a series of questions which they wish other and to ask each—the teachers. A lively discussion ensues, especially, on how tadpoles can become frogs. Here, each pupil desires to attend school! Many reference sources are utilized to secure information. To be sure, observing live tadpoles is more interesting than a formal writing activity to the teacher for grading purposes. Unless, for instance, pupils write a poem based on observations made, such as those of the above named tadpoles. Enjoyable forms of poetry such as couplets, triplets, quatrains, limericks, and haiku might then be correlated. Poetry writing which is introduced to pupils needs to meet the following standards:

- it must make sense to the student/child/pupil.
- it is introduced energetically, not in a dull and boring manner.
- it emphasizes the teacher reading aloud, with voice inflection, to bring in the interest factor in writing poetry through gestures.
- it should correlate the lesson/unit being studied, such as science/social studies.
- it should encourage good habits, and teach children to be rational.
- it may emphasize individual work, collaboration, and/or class as a whole endeavors with respect and acceptance of others being in evidence (See Rojas and Manning, 2011).

In addition to interest factors to encourage school attendance, the classroom teacher also must emphasize relevancy as a key concept in teaching. How can learnings be made relevant? The learner must perceive that what is achieved is significant. The toad/frog population is going downhill in number, and there needs to be a balance in the ecosystem. Pupils might consider this as a problem area in answer to the query, 'Why?' Gathering information from computer sources, etc. can provide relevant information. This aids pupils in broadening their horizons in thinking about animal life and its relationship to the environment. When relating poetry as another avenue of communication, the learner expands the scope of learning. As units and lessons progress, pupils will notice more avenues of vital ways of written communication such as write-ups of science experiments, reports, summaries, outlines, diary entries, logs, etc. Integrating content being studied with diverse communication skills is vital. Interesting and fascinating experiences in school improve school attendance (Kumar, 2011).

Teachers must plan and involve pupils in ongoing experiences of learnings. With purpose, learners perceive the need for learning. Thus, one perceives purpose in reading a novel to see how it ends. There could be much suspense more in reading. Also, one may feel a need to read during the day and that purpose may be for sheer enjoyment. Enjoyable experiences in reading may include sustained silent reading. During a given time, pupils are free to select a library book of their very own choice. These books might pertain to amphibians and reptiles. A highly exciting discussion followed in the writer's supervision of a university class when pupils present information in the ongoing lesson pertaining to what had been read. The content came solely from a library book. Pupils tend to want to come to school when the learning activities are interesting as well as exciting. This cuts down on absences and tardiness!

There is, also, a plethora of specific ways to emphasize pupil regular attendance in school. If, on the average, 10 per cent of the pupils are absent/tardy on a given school day, the names of these pupils must be available to make home calls to ascertain reasons for this occurrence. Alarm clocks may need to be furnished at homes where these chronic problems exist. Parents must assist children to get up on time so they are ready to get on the school bus or walk to school (if the distance is short). Programmed messages might be sent to the houses as wakeup calls. There are numerous ways to remind parents of the importance of children being in school on time. Some of them are necessary:

- sending a brochure a homes on the importance of educating children. E-mails and letters should also be sent periodically.
- presenting relevant information at parent/teacher conferences, as well as at open house pertaining to the importance of coming to school and on time.
- the school district shorting up and modifying weaknesses of present day policies on regular school attendance.

Conclusion

Regular pupil attendance is important since they lose sequential study and therefore progress, if there are absences with no reason. Parents need continual reminders of how important this is. Whatever a learner loses out on, he/she must be assisted in closing the gap. If this is not taken care of, then a pupil regresses in achievement.

REFERENCES

Ediger, Marlow (2008), "Mental Health in the Curriculum," *Journal of Instructional Psychology*, 35 (1), 38-42.

Kindervater, Terry (2010), "Models of Parent Involvement," *the Reading Teacher*, 63(7), 610-613.

Kumar, Satish (2011), "Mental Health and School Satisfaction of Truant and Non-truant Secondary School Students," *Edutracks*, 11 (4), 14-16.

Rojas, Virginia, and Emily Manning (2011), "Creating Poems from Science Research," *Reading Today*, 29 (2), 12-13.

Rodgers, Lisa, and Belinda Basca (2011), "T'was the Start of Science Notebooking," *Science and Children*, 49, (3), 56-61.

5

Need to Develop Listening Habit

The art of listening definitely needs improvement and teachers, regardless of academic subject matter taught, must aid pupils in listening achievement. Good listening habits are important in schools, but also in society. A lot of times, in oral conversation in the social arena where a participant may be embarrassed to have content repeated due to faulty listening. What might the classroom teacher do to increase listening comprehension?

Improving Listening Comprehension

The teacher needs to make sure that readiness exists for listening, prior to provide a lesson presentation. Thus, pupils must put away all unneeded objects from their desks, prior to lesson engagement. Playing with objects distracts from quality listening. Curbing unnecessary noises is important so that better listening might result. Essential standards of conduct should be developed and posted in the classroom. Teachers and pupils having understanding in implementing tenets of Emotional Intelligence (El) find it to be significant, always (Nazareth, 2010). Distracting behaviour, such as rudeness and put downs can also be evaluated in terms of these standards, and humane penalties used for each infracture should be meted out, possibly in terms of taking away a privilege.

Background information (Ausubel, 1958) must be provided to pupils to benefit from a taken up lesson. When pupils participate in an ongoing task, the teacher notices what facts, concepts and ideas learners possess and helps to fill in the gaps. Listening quality occurs when pupils possess the necessary advanced organizers in acquiring content from lesson presentation. There is an overload of information unless crucial ideas are noted and separated from the less important ideas, through careful listening.

In the new lesson, the teacher must plan to actively engage pupils in learning. A hands on approach, such as the project method helps in these endeavours. Not all activities can be handed on however, so the teacher needs to plan to have an exciting discussion, where all participate wholeheartedly. Enthusiasm is essecial to get a good habit of listening.

Second, it is important to avoid repetition while communicating orally. It does not mean avoiding review and practice, but the teacher may avoid repetition in oral statements by having pupils notice directions, for example, that can be obtained from a white board or chalkboard, if the pupil does not get it the first time. However, directions and oral content must be presented clearly in ways that pupils understand. The writer noticed carelessly given directions for an activity with clarity lacking, while supervising universities. Pupils then could not proceed with extended leanings. This has to be avoided (Ediger and Rao, 2011).

Third, pupils need to experience what is meaningful. Subject matter/skills must be presented in ways that make sense to learners. Too often, teachers rush in activities and try to cover too much ground in a small period of time. This is opposite of pupils attaching meaning to new learnings presented. Haste may certainly make for waste. Rather, the tempo and speed of learning experiences need to be such that pupils understand content, such as when a pupil repeats in his/her own words, directions are to be given by the teacher. Thus, what is taught must be taught well in which pupils understand ensuing subject matter (Ediger, 2011).

Fourth, pupils must reflect upon what has been learned. By reflecting, the pupil is assisted in recalling content acquired to notice gaps in learning. Gaps may occure due to faulty listening. Or, the learner realizes that an increased amount of knowledge is necessary. Perhaps, new interests and problems arise as a result of the reflection. Thus, identified problems need an hypothesis and modification thereof if needed, as a result of testing. Thinking about thinking is involved here (See, Listen and Zeichner, 1987). Listening carefully is essencial when engaging in cooperative problem solving.

Fifth, self efficacy is increasingly inherent if a pupil reinforces in-depth learning. Opposite of indepth is survey procedures. With in-depth learning, ideas are used again and again in new and more complex ways whereby the learner feels increasing competent in these lessons. Confidence comes from being successful. The confidence may build up in achieving degrees of self efficacy. Feeling the opposite, which is failure, hinders total development of the child such as intellectual, social, and emotional. To develop self efficacy in the child, the teacher and classmates must assist all to succeed in school and in life. Pushing, shoving, name calling, and other negative initiatives, make way for a lack of good will and feeling in the classroom as well as hindering achievement in each curriculum area. Quality listening habits depend, in part, upon respecting and helping/cooperating each other (See Goleman, 1995).

Sixth, locus of control is another important concept to emphasize teaching and learning situations. There are pupils who have some feelings on self effort making for success in achievement. Thus, the individual is responsible for doing well in coursework. Others feel that factors in the environment may determine, what transpires in life. The writer has listened to university students say, after taking a test, that the test items were faulty or did not ask for the right response. There is a member of reasons given by individuals as to why success was not at hand for any given attempt at performance. The writer has also heard students claiming, "I certainly studied hard for the exam and it paid off with the grade received." It is true that illness, fatigue, and discouragement, hinder success in school and in society. Working hard in each course has also paid off well. However, locus of control pertains to who determines what happens in life. Is it within the individual being responsible, or do external factors, beyond one's control, determine what occurs? The more successful pupils are and have been, the more likely they are to venture into the unknown with risk taking. Thus, a pupil is able to predict success in undertaking a challenging task, or he/she might avoid an ensuing experience due to the feelings of failure. This will come in degrees and not be an either/or decision with risk taking (See Rotter, 1971). Careful listening habits are crucial to become more inner self directed.

Seventh, appropriate sequence in learning is important within the framework of achieving skills in listening. Thus, the order of activities for learners to participate in, should move gradually from the less to the more complex subject. Brain hemisphere is involved here, where the left side appears to move logically in a planned sequence. The right hemisphere is creatively oriented and may perceive novelty, uniqueness, and newness without a necessarily carefully planned sequential set of activities and experiences. Art work, music, poetry writing, among others, may exemplify use of the right brain hemisphere. Intake of experiences might as well come from listening as an avenue of learning along with reading, writing, and speaking in oral communication to reveal creativity in its numerous endeavours.

Conclusion

Classroom teachers must plan lessons carefully to incorporate quality pupil listening. Incorporated objectives should include knowledge, skills, and attitudinal ends. Different learning activities in different academic areas must assist pupils to attain these ends. Evaluation needs to be frequent to notice listening progress.

REFERENCES

Ausubel, David (1958), *The Psychology of Meaningful Verbal Learning.* New York: Grune and Strattan.

Ediger, Marlow (2011), "Shared Reading, the Pupil, and the Teacher," *Reading Improvement*, 48 (2), 55-58.

Ediger, Marlow, and D. Bhaskara Rao (2011), *Essays on Teaching and Learning*. New Delhi, India: Discovery Publishing House.

Goleman, Daniel, (1995), *Emotional Intelligence*. New York: Bantam Books.

Liston, D., and Zeichner, K. (1987), "Critical Pedagogy and Teacher Education," *Journal of Teacher Education*, 169 (3), 117-137.

Nazareth, Benjamin (2010), Effect of Emotional Intelligence and Self Efficacy on B. Ed. Trainees on Their Academic Achievement. Ph D Thesis Appraised for Alagappa University, Karaikudi, India.

Rotter, Julian B. (1971), Generalized Expectancies for Interpersonal Trust," *Amorioan Psychologist*, 26 (?), 443-452.

6

Oral Communication Across the Curriculum

Proficiency in oral communication is necessary in school and in society. To do well in the different curriculum areas, pupils must speak clearly and meaningfully. For example, in a group discussion in the social studies involving the topic "the pros and cons of raising taxes," pupils need to express knowledgeable ideas with appropriate voice inflection in stress, pitch, and juncture (pauses), including a proper pace. Listeners need to be able to comprehend what is being communicated orally (semantics). The oral content may lack proper word order (syntax) which makes comprehension difficult.

The teacher must diagnose different types of errors in oral communication and provide objectives and learning opportunities which strengthen oral communication procedures (Ediger, 2011).

Teaching and Learning in Oral Communication

There is a plethora of learning opportunities involving oral communication which should assist pupils to do well in each academic area. These activities need to be goal centred. Thus, there are needed speaking skills which all need to embrace to communicate effectively. First of all, pupils need to be helped to develop oral communication skills. These are not routine, neither done for the sake of emphasizing quality communication, but rather to assist pupils to communicate effectively. The receiver must be able to find meaning to what the sender intends in communicated messages. Thus, much responsibility rests upon the pupil to send clear content. He/she must see reasons for engagement which might consist of an oral report, for example, to become a master craftsman, it involves achievement (apprentice, journey man, and master) in a unit on the Middle Ages. The learner might have selected this topic in guild membership due to personal interests in making a product of that time. Criteria such as the following, based on developmental needs, should be stressed upon emphasizing fluency on orally presented ideas:

- develop and use an outline to present sequential subject matter.
- having the subject matter fully and properly in mind when reporting to pupils.
- using voice inflection and quality pacing to encourage listening (Ediger, 2011).

Excessive criteria should not be used at one time to assist pupils in listening. A few relevant criteria may well provide the right ingredient to assist pupils in good listening habits.

Second, high pupil involvement in an activity assists learners to attend and listen carefully to the ideas of others. Thus, within a science unit of study, pupils, with teacher guidance might develop an experiment on air taking up space. Co-operative planning may include a crushed tissue paper placed inside an inverted tumbler. All need to see the occurrences clearly and raise questions when necessary. The inverted tumbler is then placed inside the classroom aquarium which is filled with water. Pupils then hypothesize as to what will happen to the crushed tissue paper. Each hypothesis is recorded pertaining to the one variable in the experiment. The teacher needs to appreciate the quality of speaking/listening (See Tichman, 2008).

Third, pupils must cultivate good human relations among pupils and the teacher. Oral communication is hindered when negative remarks are made such as inherent rudeness, put downs and downgrading of others. There are feelings involved when negative words in messages are communicated. The communicator should also notice if listeners matter are listening to notice the effectives of interacting orally with others. Assistance must be given to the pupil sending messages if there is a failure in listening. Volume may need to be increased or decreased. A pupil may not enunciate clearly thus hindering interactions. Speaking too fast or too slow also affects the quality of listening. With the teacher recording problem areas and discussing these with the involved pupil might assist in overcoming problem areas. Throughout, positive behaviours must be strengthened. Goleman (1998) has done much work the entire causes, researched and written much in researching and writing about emotional intelligence. He emphasizes the importance of empathy in dealing with others. Too often, relations are strained or broken when patience wears out. Things are then said which otherwise would not be communicated. Many people lose their jobs at the work place, not because of incompetency, but due to an unbridled tongue. Time needs to be spent on anger management. All need to control anger, lest one does something which will be dreaded in the short or long run.

Fourth, pupils need to have ample opportunities to practice quality oral communication skills. Thus, a variety of purposes in speaking need emphasis including the following:

- giving oral reports on relevant topics which capture learner interest;
- providing directions to help somebody locate a place;
- interviewing a person;
- giving an after dinner speech;
- making introductions;
- explaining how to make an object or play a game;
- participating in a reader's theater (See Tiedt).

Each speaking experience needs to possess clarity in objectives and follow recommended criteria. Rules of conduct must be followed for listeners and speakers as well. These need to be followed and appraised, periodically, by pupils with teacher guidance.

Fifth, Bandura (1997) has done much research and writing on the self efficacy concept. The major objective of self efficacy is to be motivated and competent in a plethora of situations. Efficacy in oral communication must be enhanced. Thus, to become proficient here, pupils must experience success. Failure seemingly multiplies itself and hinders growth, development, and progress. An approach that helps to develop efficacy in speaking is to have pupils achieve adequate background information, for example, in a topic being pursued in a discussion. Pupils might then, for instance, in a unit on Space Geometry, view, discuss, and draw three dimensional models of cones. Meaningfully, elaborating on the cone, and other three dimensional models, as sequential learning permits, will guide pupils achieve indepth concepts. Indepth achievement helps pupils to utilize these concepts in a variety of geometric and lifelike situations. Self efficacy develops as pupils attain increased understandings when recalling, attaching meaning to, as well as thinking critically and creatively, on related three dimensional models and objects. Opposite is survey learnings in which instruction has been hurried and shallowness in learner understandings are in evidence.

Sixth, the success model in oral communication will help pupils to take risks in being successful in a variety of situations. Rotter (1954) has worked on locus of control and in his research he came up with aiding learners who believe in the locus of control being in the environment.

What happens to the self, is largely due to external occurrences. Thus, for example, a pupil might blame receiving low grades on test questions, the teacher's method of grading, or some source other than depending upon the self. Internal locus of control, in contrast, emphasizes that pupils feel that the self is responsible such as not having studied hard for taking the test and needing to put more effort into task completion. The writer taught undergraduate and graduate university students for thirty years and heard several students comment, when receiving a low test score, that the test questions did not cover what was taught. He also remembers the time when he complained about grades received that were not fair. More time spent on study does help to receive better grades.

Conclusion

Pupils need to interact with interesting learning experiences in order to attend carefully to what is taught. Clarity in these activities is needed. Meaning and understanding in knowledge/skills should be an end result. Quality sequence, based on background information, should be in the offing. The teacher needs to provide for the many individual differences which exist among learners as well as assist each to achieve as optimally as possible in oral communication across the curriculum..

REFERENCES

Bandura, Albert. (1997), *Self Efficacy: The Exercise of Control.* New York: Freeman.

Ediger, Marlow (2011), "Shared Reading, the Pupil, and the Teacher," *Reading Improvement*, 48 (2), 55-58.

Ediger, Marlow (2011), "Leadership in the Social Studies Curriculum," *Education*,131 (4), 711-714.

Goleman, Daniel (1995), *Emotional Intelligence*. New York: Bantam Books.

Rotter, Julian B. (1954), *Social Learning Theory and Clinical Psychology.* New York: Prentice Hall.

Tichman, Evelyn (2008), "The Object of Their Attention," *Educational Leadership*, 65 (5), 44-47.

Tiedt, Iris M. (1982), *The Language Arts Handbook.* Englewood Cliffs, New Jersey.

7

Improving the Spelling Curriculum

Presently, pupils do considerable text-messaging using the latest device in wireless technology. It plays a significant role. One definitely does not want to be stuck with tradition alone. People seeming desire to possess the latest and want to communicate with others.

Spelling achievement is important for pupils in school and in society This may, also, have to do with saving the language as a standardized form (See Green and Johnson, 2010). It is appropriate to have selected guidelines for any area of study including spelling.

Spelling Words Correctly

How important is it today to be a good speller with all the available modern technology such as spell check on a computer? It is still very important since the writer must have spelled a word correctly, otherwise spell check will not be able to provide a correct spelling for the desired word. Then too, technology is not always available when writing to communicate as in a personal letter or business letter. Should there be a formal list of weekly words for pupils to conquer? Although not being a perfect procedure, the list does provide a systematic procedure in studying the correct spelling of selected words. Even then, spelling does relate closely to reading as a curriculum area. Hopefully, these are practical and functional (See Lehr, 2003).

Methods utilized in learning to spell words correctly, will, in part, determine which words are to be emphasized. Thus, words need to have a utilitarian purpose. When supervising student teachers, the writes noticed words for pupil mastery which were far removed of being useful in written work. Pupils should study the correct spelling of words which they use in communicating with others. The list could be individualized and pertain to those words a pupil misspelled in functional written work. The learner may then choose which approach to use in practicing the correct spelling. There are learners who want to spell each word correctly by writing it a number of times. There comes a problem which is that the pupil may write each word incorrectly five or ten times. If the pupil continually checks the spelling of each written word with a model; this avoids practicing a word incorrectly in writing.

Pupils may also work in dyads in practising the correct spelling of a given set of words. Thus, one of the two might say a word and the other spell that word in written form which might include word processor use. The dyad roles may be reversed until mastery occurs (See Alderman and Green, 2011).

A carefully selected spelling textbook has certain advantages for use in the classroom in that a weekly list of words is provided with an accompanying lesson plan for each day of the week. The teacher may supplement with additional activities such as

- having pupils write a poem or essay containing these words
- doing a teacher developed cross word puzzle from the weekly spelling list

- learning to spell additional words as challenge or bonus words
- adding rhyming words for words contained in the weekly list
- locating words which begin with the same beginning sound or ending sound as those in the list in addition to other phonic activities. Above all develop quality attitudes with interesting and meaningful experiences (See Gentry, 2004).

Pupils need to attach meaning involving each word encountered in an ensuing lesson. If a pupil studies the correct spelling of a word without meaning attached, the memorization process tends to be futile. Mere rote learning is then involved which will soon be forgotten. For each introduced new word, the pupil should be able to pronounce it correctly and as well as use it in one or more sentences, orally in writing.

Learners need to perceive purpose in mastering a list of words in spelling. With purpose, pupils perceive reasons for participating in the ongoing activity. This may be indicated with a reason for writing such as doing a written invitation for a birthday party or a thank you notice for a favour received. New words for spelling might well come from what is needed in each written purpose. Learners may then notice that utilitarian reasons are involved in ongoing activities (Ediger, 2011).

Individual differences must be provided in what is expected from each learner. The number of words to be mastered in a certain interval of time depends upon pupil ability and interest. Interest must be encouraged; when too much is required, pupils may become less involved and actually feel discouraged. The other extreme is a lack of challenge whereby too little is emphasized in achievement. There needs to be high, reasonable expectations of each child. Methods of instruction, too, might be dull, repetitious, and boring.

Diagnosis and remediation play an important role in the spelling curriculum. The following need analyzation:

- If adequate emphasis is placed upon phonics when words are being spelled. Selected words are spelled phonetically or there are parts of a word consistent between symbol and sound.
- If too much stress is being placed on phonics whereby the pupil spells words phonetically, but these do not follow a sound/symbol relationship. Thus, some words minimize consistency between symbol and sound (See Vijaykumar, 2011).

Words misspelled should be put on a word wall; many pupils during leisure moments look at these words and become interested in spelling words correctly. Words possess a fascination of their very own and pupils, with teacher enthusiasm, might well become intrigued with them. A variety of quality methods of instruction may develop, increasingly, feelings of self efficacy within learners. Spelling and reading are definitely related. As the reader will notice above that pupils do study phonetic analysis in spelling and these learnings should transfer to reading of subject matter or narrative content. As pupils read content, they are learning to spell new words or review those already known. Separate time should be provided for pupil independent reading in which pupils choose reading materials of personal interest. This should assist pupils to become better readers as well as spellers. Interest is a powerful factor in the reading/spelling connection.

Conclusion

Technology has stepped in to take care of selected difficulties in written work. There are educators who favour minimizing the studying of words in spelling. To be sure, technology has taken care of time consumed in composing ideas, as well as stamping and mailing letters. One, for example, does not have to worry about stamps, among other things. In written letters, the writer may think of what to write prior to sending the contents. It still may not convey the intended message since interpretation is involved by the receiver. Letters might also be saved for posterity and future research by an intended researcher of a major problem area. The author feels that spelling in written work must emphasize the philosophy of pragmatism and thus be:

- useful in communicating with others;
- meaningful in that messages make sense;
- purposeful in that reasons exist for ongoing communication;
- interesting in that wholehearted involvement provides intrinsic fulfillment;
- developing good attitudes as an end result!

REFERENCES

Alderman, Gary L, and Susan K. Green (2011), "Fostering Lifelong Spellers Through Meaningful Experiences," *The Reading Teacher*, 64 (8), 599-605.

Ediger, Marlow (2008), "Mental Health and the Curriculum," *Journal of Instructional Psychology*, 35 (1), 38-42.

Ediger, Marlow (2011), "Shared Reading, the Pupil, and the Teacher," *Reading Improvement*, 48 (1), 55-58.

Gentry, J. R. (2004), *The Science of Spelling.* Portsmouth, New Hampshire: Heinemann.

Green, S. K., and R. L Johnson 2011), *"Assessment is Essential,"* New York; McGraw Hill.

Lehr, Judy Brown (2003), "Using Learner Centred Education to Prepare Teachers for Ethical Leadership," *Education*, 124 (1), 55-62.

Vijaykumar, R. (2011), "Technology: A Catalyst of Teaching-Learning Process," *Edutracks*, 18 (11), 3-5. Published in India.

8

Portfolios in the Mathematics Curriculum

Portfolios might well be an excellent approach for pupils and mathematics teachers to share the former's achievement with parents, as well as with other interested, responsible persons. Here, parents may observe and evaluate pupil progress authentically. Parents then may view learner achievement directly from pupil products, not from test scores. Questions arise and answers given in assessing the products. The valid concerns of parents might become a part of the portfolio.

A plethora of mathematics products may become a part of the portfolio. They represent efforts, motivation, and pupil purposes in ongoing lessons and units of study. Here, the pupil is actively engaged in choosing what to include in a portfolio. He/she is not a passive recipient, but evaluates, learns, grows and develops in the process. Too frequently, pupils merely respond to test items given on the local, state, and national levels. From test results, the pupil passively views a percentile, grade equivalent, or per cent given for correct answers given. In doing a portfolio, the pupil selects representative inclusions. It is flexible and open ended in terms of its development (See Kasinath, 2009).

Philosophy of Portfolio Development

Constructivism, as a psychology of learning, emphasizes that the pupil is in charge of his/her learning activities. As an active learner, the pupils sequences his/her own experiences. The mathematics teacher is a facilitator and guide, not a lecturer. He/she observes and assists pupils to learn by discovery. The mathematics teacher sets the stage in introducing new subject matter. New learnings are developed by pupils in moving from the known to the unknown. If a learner needs help on a new process in mathematics, the teacher raises questions which lead pupils to the correct response. Telling is not teaching, but scaffolding based on background information guides each pupil to achieve more optimally. Thus, the pupil develops his/ her own knowledge within a learning sequence (Ediger, 2010).

Constructivism emphasizes the uniqueness of the learner with his/her own background knowledge and culture. Responsibility for achieving in mathematics resides within the pupil.The teacher encourages each pupil to achieve in mathematics, but motivation is intrinsic and comes from within the learner. Teaching is facilitating learning and there is a dynamic interaction among the learning activity, the mathematics teacher, and the pupil. For example, within an ongoing unit of study pertaining to place value, properties of four basic operations, fractions, decimals, regrouping and renaming, estimation, statistics and probability, as well as fundamental learnings in algebra and geometry, the pupil together with the facilitator, and curriculum interact; they are not separate entities (See Wolk, 2008).

Testing is very frequently used to ascertain pupil achievement in mathematics. Here, the learner is a somewhat passive individual, responding to multiple choice test items. Portfolio develop emphasizes the learner being actively involved in choosing entries from daily work completed within lessons and units of study. A random sampling is chosen by the pupil with teacher facilitation. A Table of Contents brings order to these dated entries and makes it easier for parents, teachers, and other responsible individuals to peruse and evaluate mathematical learnings developed by a pupil. The following are examples of what may become a part of a mathematics portfolio:

- daily work completed in ongoing lessons and units of study;
- line, bar, and circle graphs as well as charts made such as a narrative which tells the history of number and its uses, a tabulation chart which indicates growth and comparisons in population figures of selected countries integrated with the social studies, an organizational chart indicating structure and order in base ten numeration, and pictured graphs in chart form, among others;
- objects constructed such as a place value chart, a fact finder, beanstalks to show sets of different values, and a fraction/decimal chart;
- games developed such as addition, subtraction, and multiplication bingo;
- electronic photos of constructed items such as geoboards and tangrams;
- drawings of geometrical models, attribute blocks, as well as other manipulative materials;
- recordings of pupils involved in small group discussions (Ediger, 2005).

The above are examples of what might constitute a portfolio of pupil work and products. Active pupil involvement necessitates the choosing of contents for the portfolio. He/she owns the portfolio and shares its selection of entries with the facilitator/teacher. The portfolio, too, provides a basis for doing parent/teacher conferences. Here, the learner may play a leadership role in discussing achievement within the conference. What has been accomplished and what is left to learn is diagnostic as well as remedial and promotes developmental learnings.

Somewhat opposite of constructivism and portfolio development is behaviourism. Behaviourism stresses the following:

- establishing measurable objectives for pupils to attain in mathematics;
- aligning learning opportunities with the stated objectives;
- teaching toward pupils attaining these objectives (Ediger, 2003).

A deductive approach is generally used in teaching mathematics. Content moves from the teacher to pupils with the end result being for the latter to achieve behaviourally stated objectives. Testing is a major procedure used to ascertain pupil progress. Pupil results are indicated through precise numerical results such as percentiles and grade equivalents (See Gardner, 1993).

Constructivism, Dewey, Piaget, and Vygotsky

Three highly recognized constructivists are John Dewey, Jean Piaget, and Len Vygotsky. Dewey (1916) emphasized a problem solving curriculum whereby the pupil with teacher guidance would identify a problem within a unit of study. Pupils need to have necessary background information to delve into securing a possible solution. The problem needs adequate delimitation so that it can be solved. There are a plethora of practical problems in mathematics which need to be identified. These require deliberation and thought, not a factual answer. For example, a classroom is securing new carpeting. The problem then pertains to securing the number of square feet or square yards for the covering. Pupils initially might hypothesize how to ascertain the approximate answer. They are actively involved here as they are in sequential steps of solving a problem. The teacher may raise questions as needed to assist pupils in mathematical problem solving. After deliberation, pupils may check their hypothesis of necessary skills to ascertain the answer as well as evaluate the correctness of the answer. There is interaction, here, between the pupil, the teacher, and the curriculum. This might be an individual or small group endeavour.

Jean Piaget (1973) stressed a maturation theory of learning whereby the pupil develops different capabilities of thought as he/she progresses in age and through the grades in school. There were four stages of pupil development as Piaget's research indicated:

- sensori-motor, ages birth to eighteen months of age
- pre-operational, eighteen months to seven years
- concrete operations, seven to eleven years of age
- formal operations, twelve years and older

In each of the above named years, pupils change and modify their perceptions. Thus, from birth to eighteen months of age, pupils need to experience concrete objects and items. Learning occurs through viewing, interacting, and observing. In the pre-operational stage, the pupil also experiences the concrete, but perceives each by seeing one variable at a time. The stage of concrete operations emphasizes blending the concrete with increasingly more abstract learnings such as physical representations with numbers/numerals. Whereas, the stage of formal operations stresses that pupils can reason through abstract methods in using numbers/numerals in addition, multiplication, subtraction, and division. Reasoning and inventing have become leading approaches in learning as well as critical, creative thinking, and problem solving. Piaget emphasized that individually the pupil arrived at each stage maturationally and was assisted through each stage with adult/teacher guidance.

Vygotsky emphasized that learning was a social situation, not individually based. Thus, within a committee or small group pupils worked together on a project. Members learn from each other when interacting and ideas "bounce off the minds" of participants. The teacher facilitates learning among group members, but does not, by any means, dominate the participation. The small group progresses with active participation and ideas are modified within the committee. By challenging and modifying ideas presented, committee members benefit in developing comprehensive structures (See Vygotsky, 1978).

Commonalities in psychological/philosophical thinking involving John Dewey, Jean Piaget, and ten Vygotsky are the following:

- the teacher is a facilitator of learning and not a 'sage on the stage';
- pupils own the curriculum with the teacher assisting learner achievement and progress;
- pupils construct knowledge and acquisition does not come from lecture or the teacher indoctrinating with what is correct;
- sequence in achieving resides within the pupil, not the materials of instruction;
- pupils interact among themselves, the materials of instruction, and the teacher. There is interaction not domination. With the thinking of Jean Piaget, however, the pupil develops largely through maturation

REFERENCES

Dewey, John (1916), *Democracy in Education*. New York: The MacMillan Company.

Ediger, Marlow (2010), "Portfolios in Science," *Virginia Journal of Science Education*, 3(2), 12.

Ediger, Marlow (2005), "Teaching Mathematics in the School Setting," *College Student Journal*, 39(4), 711-715.

Ediger, Marlow (2003), *Teaching Mathematics Successfully*. New Delhi, India: Discovery Publishing House.

Gardner, Howard (1993), *Multiple Intelligences: Theory Into Practice*. New York: Basic Books.

Kasinath, H. M. (2009), "Nature of Knowledge in Constructivism, Implications for Education," *Journal of Community Guidance and Research*, 26 (3), 259-266.

Piaget, Jean (1973), *To Understand is to Invent*. New York: Grossman.

Vygotsky, Len S. (1978), *Mind In Society*. Cambridge, Massachusetts: Harvard University Press.

Wolk, S. (2008), "Joy in School," *Educational Leadership*, 66 (1), 8-14.

9

Assisting Pupils in Mathematics Achievement

Mathematics teachers must expect reasonably high standards of achievement from pupils. Too frequently, pupils attain at a substandard level and more optimal achievement is necessary. Thus, pupils should have self esteem needs met in the school and classroom setting. Thus, learners feel that mathematics is worthwhile and effort must be put forth to accomplish and grow to achieve objectives. With the common core objectives and tests, teachers need to align the subject matter taught with the proposed ends of instruction. Each pupil needs to have help, as necessary, from the teacher as well as from peers to achieve objectives, in the common core. A collaborative environment must be in the offing so that pupils feel confident of trust and empathy being in the offing (Ediger and Rao, 2011).

The Common Core

The teacher should have high expectations for learner progress in mathematics. These expectations must be reasonable. Pupils can be aided to attain at a higher level with scaffolding. Here, the maths teacher notices the present achievement level of each pupil and when difficulties arise, assists the learners with intermediate explanations to move from the present to a bar set upward. Knowledgeable and skillful teachers are able to do this to realize more optimal pupil achievement. With getting to know each pupil's level of attainment, the teacher might well be able to secure an upward level of progress with quality instruction, and this includes scaffolding. The focal point is upon the child and his/her present status in mathematics and through scaffolding realize an optimal level (National Council Teachers of Mathematics, 2000).

Effort, not native ability and aptitude, is salient to consider in teaching. The writer has heard children state that "Mathematics is just not my cup of tea, and my parents were the same way." Here, the problem is justification for lower achievement and a lack of effort put forth to reach out and attain vital objectives. Jerome Bruner wrote, "Any subject matter can be learned in some intellectually honest form by a child at any stage of development." The concern here is "in some intellectually honest form," indicating that it must harmonize with the learner's present level of attainment before moving on to more complex key facts, concepts, and generalizations. The structure of mathematics is then a focal point of teaching, not trivia nor the irrelevant. Mathematics can also be highly practical as well as utilitarian for pupils (See NCTM 2003).

Positive attitudes must be infused in pupil thinking in that he/she can do mathematics well. Learners then need to experience success in learning. They need to be able to explain a new process acquired in their very own words; the teacher might then diagnose misunderstandings and that which needs further elaboration. Formative assessments given during the time a unit is taught also provides feedback in terms of what is lacking in mastery learning. A good teacher is a reputable diagnostician (Ediger, 1989).

Providing for diverse styles of learning is salient. By doing this, pupils have better opportunities to achieve objectives in mathematics and in the common core. The following are some of the considerations in emphasizing learning styles:

- working by the self or doing assignments collectively in committees;
- inductive *versus* deductive activities;
- heavy use of teacher explanations *versus* constructivism;
- cognitive objectives stressed solely, as compared to affective/attitudinal goals in the mathematics curriculum;
- teachers sequencing pupil progress in mathematics *versus* rather heavy learner involvement in ascertaining order of experiences;
- carefully selected textbook use in determining the math curriculum as compared to heavy infusion of problem solving experiences (Ediger, 2006).

The common core test results then may be upped by teachers paying careful attention to individual learning styles. In all situations involving maths instruction, the teacher must have a positive attitude toward that curriculum area. This conveys to learners the saliency of mathematics in school and in society.

At the end of daily instruction in mathematics, pupils should periodically be asked ."What did you learn today in mathematics?" These comments may be recorded on the white board and a copy sent home with each pupil for parental observation and comment. Too frequently, parents/guardians do not hear about daily pupil progress in mathematics. Communication, here, needs to go beyond parent/teacher conferences, as well as report cards. Parents/guardians should be invited to comment on the daily notices sent home. The question arises, "What can the home setting do to assist the learner in maths achievement involving the common core?" Quality communication between home and school is a necessity for pupil performance in mathematics and be ongoing. Both home and school must be strong advocates of and believe that children can do well in mathematics. Praise and support of math achievement must be in the offing. Realizing common core objectives should aid pupils to do well in school and in society (NCTM, 1989).

Learning experiences in mathematics need to incorporate content from the best research studies stressing more optimal learner progress. The research must have emphasized random sampling of groups involved in these studies with valid and reliable measurement instruments used. The question arises in what makes for quality in a well designed study. Maths teachers must have access to these research results, as well as to educational journals and university textbooks pertaining to improving the school curriculum. In service education for mathematics teachers need to incorporate

- school and system wide meetings in discussing problems in teaching
- attending professional conferences, state and national, devoted to improving mathematics teaching
- discussions based on reading content from professional materials in mathematics instruction
- taking advanced courses in mathematics education from colleges and universities
- speaking at mathematics conferences on a selected facet of teaching
- interacting with a colleague in talking about ways he/she has experienced in helping students succeed in mathematics (See, NCTM, 2001).

Daily time devoted to teaching mathematics should be adequate in duration which includes conferences with learners. Thus, pupils may reflect upon what has been learned as well as achieve ensuing vital ideas emphasizing the common core. Putting new learnings to use helps to reinforce what has been acquired as well as aid in retention of subject matter. Improved attitudes might well result if pupils truly understand structural mathematical content as well as perceive its utilization in school and in society. Pupils sometimes ask how will these learnings be of personal benefit to them. The maths teacher needs to justify the importance of each lesson plan and its implementation. Difficulties faced by pupils need identification and meaningful instruction follow. The proficient teacher has a repertoire of procedures available to assist learner progress.

Mentoring might also be practiced in that an experienced teacher may assist a beginning teacher in teaching mathematics. Quality human relations need to be in the offing whereby the inexperienced teacher increasingly develops feelings of self efficacy whereby in the succeeding years of teaching mathematics, he/she becomes more knowledgeable of subject matter/skills, thus revealing confidence as well as competence. The experienced maths teacher, too, benefits from mentoring in that he/she:

- benefits in learning more about content and skills, necessary to truly being a professional;
- profits from discussing problems pertaining to the classroom setting, involving math instruction;
- has social needs met in working with others in teaching mathematics (See Wiske, 2004).

Conclusion

The mathematics teacher provides a vital role in guiding pupil progress in meeting common core standards. The mathematics curriculum needs to reflect more optimal achievement in the common core. In the meantime, each day of instruction is salient and provides background knowledge and skills for successive levels of progress. Research findings and the psychology of learning have much to offer in teaching and learning situations. A quality background of mathematical knowledge and procedures in teaching are necessary to develop feelings of self efficacy and competency in instruction. Pupils need to make sense and attach meaning in ingoing mathematical experiences. They must learn to reason abstractly and quantitatively, as well as to be able to justify their thinking to others. Models need to be used in mathematical thinking. There are a variety of learning opportunities as well as tools available in emphasizing precision in securing information and answers. Thus, the common core provides an effective curriculum in mathematics to help ensure that major ideas are secured.

REFERENCES

Cuban, Larry (2006), *"The Perennial Reform: Fixing School Time,"* Phi Delta Kappan, 90 (4), 240-250.

Ediger, Marlow, and D. Bhaskara Rao (2011), *Essays on Teaching Mathematics.* New Delhi, India: Discovery Publishing House.

Ediger, Marlow (1989), *"Psychology of Teaching Mathematics,"* Delta K, 27 (4), 20-23.

Ediger, Marlow (2006), "Teaching Mathematics in the High School Setting," *College Student Journal,* 39 (4) 711-715).

National Council Teachers of Mathematics (2000), *Principles and Standards for School Mathematics.* Reston, Virginia: NCTM.

NCTM (1989), *Curriculum and Evaluation Standards for School Mathematics.* Reston, Virginia: NCTM.

NCTM (2003). *A Research Companion for Principles and Standards for School Mathematics.* Reston, Virginia: NCTM.

NCTM (2001), *Adding It All Up: Helping Children Learn Mathematics.* Reston, Virginia: NCTM.

Wiske, L. (2004), "Technology to Dig for Meaning," *Educational Leadership,* 63 (1), 478-488.

Teaching Science and English Language Learners

With the increase in English Language Learners (ELL) in the public schools, it behooves professional teachers to update skills in teaching. This includes the science curriculum which is pinpointed in this manuscript. ELL pupils come from homes where English is not spoken at all or is not the dominant language. States have requirements here as to who to include as ELL learners. There are criteria for teachers to use in teaching science to this category of pupils in order to optimize learning:

- subject matter must be meaningful so that pupils understand what is taught;
- interest is learning is vital and is inherent if learning is to occur;
- purpose in learning is highly significant; otherwise pupils may not perceive value in achieving objectives within ongoing lessons and units in science;
- learning styles vary within learners in terms of how science is taught;
- individual differences must be provided for since pupils differ in science achievement.

Teaching English Language Learners in Science

The science teacher needs to ascertain the present level of achievement of each learner in English as well as in the science unit being taught. This is necessary for the pupil to progress from the known to the unknown. Being ready for the ensuing is salient. Thus the science teacher must plan learning opportunities based on what the ELL knows and what is left to learn. Once this has been ascertained, he/she needs to implement resulting plans. For example, the science teacher may develop an experiment, in a science unit of study involving 'evaporation,' which all can see clearly in order to benefit from instructional procedures. Depending upon where these learners are in achievement, the teacher may point to the aquarium and pronounce its related abstract word 'aquarium'. Pupils here may also say the same word to reinforce what is being learned. This word may be posted in the classroom word wall. Thus, to show what happens to the water in the aquarium, the science teacher needs to mark the present water level. Pupils are encouraged to view the level of the water periodically. Understandable words are used to explain what to observe. Meaningful communication must take place. ELL pupils will, of course, notice that the water in the aquarium is going below the mark. This may be discussed in clear terminology. Why did the water go below the marked level? The writer observed the following given answers:

- the fish drank the water;
- the aquarium leaks;
- water was taken from the aquarium (See Kehr, 2009).

Each of these hypotheses is discussed, such as taking a paper towel to show no leakage occurred. However, for the hypothesis of "fish drinking the water," the teacher may then use a glass quart jar, filled to the top with water. The water level is marked. ELL pupils may then notice, "There are no fish to drink the water." Periodically, pupils also observe that no water is taken from the jar at any time. They will observe the water level going below the marked level. If pupils fail to come up with an hypothesis, the teacher needs to write the word 'evaporation' on the word wall, followed by a clear, concise explanation. At this point, ELL need to visit the school's playground on a particular day to notice a water puddle, followed by the water having evaporated the next day. It may not always be possible to notice all variables in one experiment. These experiments can bring to the ELL attention, of the water cycle. A published illustration or one dawn by the teacher might well be utilized for the explanation and discussion. Securing the interests and active involvement of ELL are paramount. They are greatly needed to optimize learning. All learning must be made as concretely as possible with objects and items used in experiments together with clarity in related discussions (See National Research Council, 1996).

Sequentially, pupils may clearly observe a related experiment, whereby one variable also is tested, pertaining to two potted plants from the same/similar stock. The word 'plant(s)' is shown on the word wall with an accompanying illustration. Pupils, too, notice that:

- the same soil is used in planting for both pots. The words 'soil' and 'pots' are pointed to when being identified on the word wall
- the same recommended amount of fertilizer is used for both
- the same amount of water, observed by pupils, is added to each pot
- the same amount of sunlight for each setting on the window sill (Ediger 2007).

Now, pupils hypothesize what will happen if one of the two plants is covered with a paper sack. They can observe each plant carefully and not jump to hasty conclusions. Writing up each experiment is salient, indicating what happened through observation and relating it to the original hypothesis The next experiment may stress that one potted plant receives adequate water, while the other receives no water. Pupils then hypothesize and observe what is happening. For ELL, an experience chart may be written to summarize what happened in these experiments. Pupils present the content orally while the teacher records the content. Learners may see their own ideas recorded on the white wall. They are read aloud together with teacher guidance as he/she points to each word in the read aloud. Here, pupils are expanding their sight word vocabulary in reading meaningful content pertaining to the science experiment. An authentic, clearly visible, experiment with related words read aloud pertaining to the hypothesis is noticed as talk written down. The experience chart may be reread, as often as desired, thus aiding ELL in recognizing words in print. Reading aloud without teacher assistance is recommended once pupils develop feelings of security in reading the contents of the science experiment. This helps pupils in understanding the methods of science in conducting experiments as well as in reading subject matter.

During story hour, the teacher might read, orally, selected library books in science on the understanding level of ELL. The library books, in this situation, should relate to the science unit being taught. The first unit discussed above dealt with the concept of 'evaporation,' whereas the second dealt with plant needs including water. By reading aloud during story hour those library books which relate to the science experiments, pupils are expanding their knowledge and skills of relevant content. Vital questions may be raised by the teacher to stimulate learning and provide opportunities for oral communication skills. Relating subject matter helps ELL to retain ideas longer as compared to isolated content (Ediger, 2008).

The examples provided above assist ELL to perceive relationships in reading activities as well as in experimentation. Additional science activities for ELL are the following:

- reading developmentally appropriate library books to expand leanings in ongoing lessons and units of study. These may also be read within a small committee whereby pupils help each other as needed in word recognition and meaning. The teacher monitors and assists as needed;

- reading subject matter from the adopted basal science textbook. The teacher reads aloud the first time while ELL follow along in their textbook. Pupils, when ready, may read aloud together the same selection. Questions and their respective answers need elaboration to check for understanding and to provide learners opportunities to practice using the English language. Scaffolding may be provided by the teacher whereby the learner may understand more complex ideas;
- viewing and listening to discussions on videotape pertaining to content in an ongoing lesson/unit of study. ELL need many opportunities to practice the use of English in different functional learning experiences;
- science words posted on the word wall may be reviewed and used in sentences. The teacher may model proper sentence structure as is necessary;
- journal writing needs to be stressed which is on the achievement level of ELL. The dated entries may be constructed by the group, typed by the teacher in a word processor and viewed on a large screen, and then copied in their respective journals. As growth in writing continues, ELL might well become increasingly independent in writing as sequential learnings progress;
- hands on approaches are useful since this emphasizes concrete learning situations while abstract ideas are read and discussed relating directly to what is being constructed.

There are selected principles of learning which need to be stressed when teaching ELL. The following are strongly recommended:

- objectives must be developmentally appropriate for the level of English and science content possessed;
- sequence in learning needs to be approached from the child's present achievement level. The science teacher should carefully observe when the sequence is too complex or too easy;

- subject matter in science must be understood with meaning attached. The quality of ELL response to questions raised becomes a gauge to instruction;
- interest, developed and maintained in ongoing lessons and units of study is a prime motivator of learning;
- purpose in learning needs to be established for each science objective to be attained. Thus, learning is not for the sake of doing so but relevant reasons are involved.

Concrete materials must be used in teaching and learning situations as is utilized in experimentation. The materials used here can be observed with the English language attached to each during instruction which makes it possible for ELL to achieve and progress. Success in learning is salient. In addition to, or in place of non-available concrete materials, pictures and illustrations help ELL to make sense of the English language and thus understand science subject matter.

Portfolios and Science

ELL find it very suitable to develop portfolios to reveal what has been accomplished in science. They may then select which entries should go into the portfolio. The entries emphasize authenticity in that ELL products are shown. The science teacher is a guide and facilitator, not a determiner. There are a plethora of entries from which to choose. Portfolio development is a philosophy of evaluation. Too frequently, tests are used to ascertain ELL progress. However, testing has its many weaknesses:

- it attempts to measure objectively basic knowledge and skill which pupils should have achieved. It has always been complex to ascertain what these basics are since human beings write the test items;
- then too, objectivity is a difficult term to define with many believing it means using multiple choice test items with standardization involved in scoring, directions given for test taking, and the same test items provided for all to take on a certain grade level. However, pupils are different in abilities, interests, and purposes, among other factors;

- pupils zero in to secure the correct response in multiple choice test items. There is no leeway in being creative when responding to any multiple choice test item. This tends to stress factual recall of information in testing situations.

Portfolio development emphasizes pupil choice, with teacher assistance, in developing and choosing entries. A Table of Contents with dated products provides order and organization. The following entries may be placed within a portfolio:

- drawings and write-ups of science experiments performed;
- electronic photos of art work, models, murals, and bulletin board displays, among other projects, completed in ongoing science units of study;
- poems, summaries, essays, and book reports as a part of science lessons;
- recordings of oral book reports and class discussions.

Portfolios may be shared with the pupil's parents in a conference setting. The pupil might well introduce diverse entries to show understanding and progress. ELL then may share ownership of the portfolio with parents and other interested persons.

REFERENCES

Ediger, Marlow (2007), *School Science Education.* New Delhi, India: Discovery Publishing House.

Ediger, Marlow (2008), "Leadership in the School Setting," *Education*, 129 (1), 17-20.

Kehr, Linda (2009), "Designing Payloads," *Science and Children*, 46 (9), 22-26.

National Research Council (1996), *National Science Education Standards.* Washington, DC: National Academy Press.

11

Which Plan of Reading Instruction is Best?

Which is the very best plan of reading instruction? There are a plethora of plans available to assist pupils to achieve more optimally. A major problem is to match the reading plan with the learner. Pupils need to accept and benefit from the chosen procedure. One size does not fit all; this expression has been used numerous times in referring to No Child Left Behind (NCLB) and is applicable to choosing a reading programme for children. The question arises, "Which plan assists pupils to best become fluent readers?"

Different Philosophies of Reading Instruction

Each recommended plan of teaching and learning has selected key beliefs. The beliefs must translate into effective programmes of teaching reading. Pupils need assistance to become good readers in decoding as well as in comprehension. The chosen plan of reading needs to harmonize with the possessed learning style (Ediger 2005).

- individualized reading stresses the pupil selecting which sequential library books to complete. Selections are based on learner interests with teacher/pupil conferences generally held after each completed book in reading. The selection of library books must be broad in genre and reading levels. What are the advantages of individualized reading?

- decision making is being emphasized by pupils. Decision making is highly salient in school and in society.
- to own the curriculum, pupils do better if choices are permitted in terms of what to read.
- teachers must have a good knowledge of children's library books in order to stress quality in conferences with pupils. Pupils are to indicate decoding and comprehension skills.
- time on task is important since pupils enjoy considerable freedom in choices made.

Disadvantages include the following:

- selected pupils are not ready to choose a library book to read nor in settling down to read.
- there are pupils who are hierarchical and want the teacher to make the choices.
- certain teachers find it difficult in being adequately knowledgeable about children's literature in order to cary out quality discussions of children's literature in conference settings with pupils.
- self discipline is difficult for the pupil in monitoring his/her own reading.

To every action, there is a somewhat equal reaction in choosing a plan of reading instruction. There are advantages and disadvantages for each. The plan adopted, in whole or in part, must meet personal needs of the individual and encourage interest in reading. Too frequently with drill and practice, interest is minimized. Much criticism has been aimed at mandated testing due to much repetitive teaching of possible skills on that test.

Basal readers have been popular over the years in teaching reading. The accompanying manual lists suggested objectives for pupil achievement, learning activities to achieve objectives, and evaluation procedures to achieve progress. The teacher may be creative in using the basal by considering it as a handbook, from which choices may be made in terms, for example, of learning activities (See Fountas and Pinnell 1999).

For the teacher, there are suggestions for teaching in the Manual. This provides a richer repertoire in curriculum development, as well as in reading instruction. The pros in using basal readers also include the following:

- beginning teachers, in particular, have security in teaching reading with the utilization of a carefully chosen basal and the accompanying Manual.
- they are written and developed by specialists in the teaching of reading.

There are always disadvantages for any plan of teaching:

- basals have not met the needs of selected pupils when providing for individual differences.
- it becomes very formal and artificial when teachers become dependent on the Manual. Authentic teaching is then lacking.

Reading teachers must adapt instruction to individual learner needs, not what a manual may say or what other reading programmes advocate. The focal point is the pupil and his/her need to become proficient in reading. When being a good reader, the pupil is able to read subject matter in the natural sciences, the social sciences, the arts, as well as content in mathematics and the other academic disciplines. The pupil needs to make sequential progress with good teaching. A developmental programme of instruction is then in evidence with room for the zone of proximal development (ZPD). The ZPD emphasizes where a pupil is presently in achievement with the reading teacher stressing a higher, possible achievable objective. That gap may be filled with quality learning activities. An issue in reading instruction pertains to a strong program of phonics for young school aged children *versus* a whole language approach. Phonics instruction is of value when integrated with meaning in comprehension. There are consistent phonic understandings when relating specific graphemes and phonemes. Many times, the reader identifies an unknown word through recognizing an initial consonant and utilizing context clues. Additional means of phonic word recognition include:

- dividing an unknown into syllables.
- dividing an unknown into shorter words (See Callow, 2008).

A Big Book approach in reading instruction might well emphasize a whole language approach in teaching reading. Thus, five to six pupil are seated around a large, interesting library book. The contents need to be clearly visible to those involved. A computer with a large screen may also be used. The teacher stimulates interest in reading by discussing the related illustrations with pupils. This is followed by the reading teacher pointing to each word read aloud, as pupils follow along carefully. The teacher needs to observe if each pupil is looking at sequential words intensively. The read aloud continues with pupils joining in. The activity may be repeated as often as desired.

Selected teachers bring in phonic learnings with asking questions such as the following:

- which words, for example, did we read which rhyme with 'man?'
- which word(s) begin with the letter 'd' as in dog?' (Lower case 'd' and 'dog' are printed on the board (Ediger 2003).

Phonic approaches should be taught based on individual pupil need. If a pupil knows selected phonic learnings, they must not be 'taught' these same learnings again. When supervising university student teachers, the writer noticed that lesson plans incorporated phonics even though these had been mastered by selected pupils. Ensuing reading objectives should be new and challenging. A workable strategy needs to be utilized to assist pupils to attain relevant learnings. Diversity of purposeful experiences must be provide for remedial and developmental teaching.

Achieving measurably stated objectives *versus* open ended goals has drawn much attention in reading instruction. Presently, measurably stated objectives is receiving emphasis. No Child Left Behind (NCLB) has emphasized testing to challenge and motivate learners to work harder. NCLB is being revised and, no doubt, will stress nationwide testing. Test results are precise and provide a number such as a percentile, or grade equivalent. This provides data for failing or promoting a pupil in moving on to the next grade level. There are a plethora of difficulties involved in having pupils take a single standardized test to notice achievement, progress, and promotional purposes (See Campbell, 2007). These include the following:

- generally, multiple choice test items are used and pupils are to choose the 'correct' response whereby the response may not be that clear cut;
- higher levels of cognition are minimized since 'correctness,' as defined by test writers, is being stressed in choosing the right answer;
- thinking outside the box is definitely discouraged. Thus, creative and critical thinking, as well as problem are greatly minimized;
- test writers, unknown to teachers and pupils, come from areas removed from the local school. This would not square with constructivism, a psychology of learning, or that the teacher needs to know pupils well and their individual capabilities to teach reading effectively;
- vast numbers of tests are machine scored and thus uniformity is emphasized in time limits for test taking, the same test items for each grade level of pupils taking the test, and the same norms for evaluating each pupil's score on the test.

Standardized tests attempt to have 'sameness' in all its contents and methods of test taking, but the major difference is that pupils differ from each other in myriad ways. Education should not standardize pupils, but be modified to provide for different interests, and abilities of learners. Pupils progress at diverse rates of speed and have different goals in life. When looking at all the listed occupations of workers in a nation, individuals truly have many choices and decisions to make. These should be made on the basis of the learner's talents and what he/she can do well with involved purposes. High school students must be assisted to make personal choices based on what is perceived salient by the student. Forcing the student to make occupational and vocational choices is to be frowned upon. Dogmatic advice also is abhorrent. Student need to be respected and valued for their own sake. Rudeness and intimidation have no roles to play in teaching, learning, and guidance services. Students are human beings with feelings, values, and attitudes. Attitudes need to be accepting of others, respectful, and polite (Bottoms 2008).

REFERENCES

Bottoms, Gene (2007), "Treat All Students Like the 'Best' Students," *Educational Leadership*, 64 (7), 30-32.

Callow, Jon (2008), "Show Me: Principles for Assessing Student's Visual Literacy," *The Reading Teacher*, 61 (8), 616-628.

Campbell, Peter (2007), *"Edison is the Symptom, NCLB is the Disease,"* Phi Delta Kappan, 438-443.

Ediger, Marlow and D. Bhaskara Rao (2003), *Teaching Reading Successfully*. New Delhi, India: Discovery Publishing House.

Ediger, Marlow and D. Bhaskara Rao (2005), *Philosophy of Education*. New Delhi, India: Discovery Publishing House.

Fountas, I. C., and G. S. Pinnell (1999), Matching Books to Readers: Using Levelled Books in Guided Reading, K-3," Portsmith, New Hampshire: Heinemann.

12

Studying Grammar in the Technological Age

When being a student in grade school as well as in high school (1934-1946), grammar was heavily emphasized in English/ language arts classes, particularly in grades four through the senior year in high school. Evidently, teachers and school administrators then saw a theoretical way to assist pupils in writing achievement. Grammar and writing were perceived as being one and the same. However, as time went on, the need was seen to stress grammar within the framework of practical, written work. Where does grammar fit in, into today's technological age with texting and cell phone utilization?

Grammar in the School Setting

There certainly are a plethora of learnings which may serve as objectives in the study of grammar integrated with diverse purposes in pupils' written work. Grammar should be functional and relevant in the lives of learners. Thus, what is acquired must be used in school and in society. Purposes are then involved in attaining objectives of instruction. Too many times, grammar has been dull and uninspiring. This need not be the case when numerous activities are provided which stimulate and motivate (Ediger and Rao, 2005). For example, learning the parts of speech might well interest many pupils if the following experiences are provided in initial and ongoing activities in understanding the concept of verbs:

- dramatize with demonstrating action such as run, jump, sing, hop, write, among others;
- do illustrations in art work pertaining to diverse actions;
- write a couplet with involved action words;
- cooperatively, pupils write free verse with action words (Ediger, 2011).

Adverbs modify verbs, as well as adjectives and other adverbs, which might also be dramatized initially, with the semi-concrete, and abstract learnings following in sequence as achievement advances:

- she walked *slowly* (It tells how she walked);
- the man spent money *lavishly;*
- the girl slept *soundly;*
- Molly ran *up the stairs* (up the stairs is an adverb phrase telling where she ran (See Tiedt, 1982).

In the last asterisked item above, up is a preposition. That word could be substituted with other prepositions such as *down* or phrases such as *in the* street. Prepositions, too, may be dramatized and indicate a relationship between the object of the preposition and another noun, such as the subject of the sentence, *e.g.* Molly and stairs. Pupils tend to enjoy playing with words, relating to a concrete situation, in that other subjects or prepositions may be used than what was given in an initial sentence. The subjects, too, may change with other parts of speech such as the pronoun. Thus, instead of 'Molly,' the pronoun she may be utilized. This, too, might be dramatized in the classroom in a concrete situation. Illustrations also may be used to show relationships of the subject and an object of the preposition such as a boy sitting in a desk; the preposition 'in' relates 'boy' with 'desk.' Other prepositions might show this relationship such as—on, in front of, behind, beside, and near. Adverb phrases which begin as prepositions but also have an object, such as those previously mentioned above, provide excellent opportunities for pupils to study the concept of misplaced modifiers. Would it be correct to say, "In his desk, the boy sat?" It does make sense, however, there appears to be a more acceptable word order—The boy sat in the desk. Perhaps, some would argue that "The boy sat in a chair adjacent to the desk." Word order, syntax, is salient in writing due to many errors in interpretation being possible. Adjective phrases, especially, are susceptible to misplacement. For instance, "The boy rode the bicycle with a read scarf," might be subjected to the following question: Did the boy or the bicycle have the red scarf? Usually, syntactically, it wold be the boy. Thus, the adjective clause should follow, "The boy with the red scarf, since it modifies 'boy,' not bicycle. Word order, or syntax, would indicate this to be the case. In very rare situations would the "The bicycle with the red scarf," be true. In some situations, it does not matter as much with word order, such as in the following: "The horse ran into the barn," or "Into the barn, the horse ran." Although, the former would be much more acceptable, conventionally. Semantics deals with what the meaning is of the communique. The sentence may be grammatically correct, but it needs interpretation and thus written more precisely (Kanti, 2011).

Noun, adjective, and adverb clauses sequentially, should be taught on the secondary level, or middle school level if readiness permits. Learners need to develop a good attitude toward grammar whereby it is not pushed down the throats of pupils, but readiness is there to profit from its study. A study of grammar must be interesting and result in improved written work. The writer would like to have the following discussed by faculty members in a school to ascertain if/when they should be taught to improve pupil's activities in composition:

- labelling above each or some words in selected sentences if it is a noun, pronoun, adjective, adverb, preposition, conjunction, or interjection. Interjections, for example, are relatively easy to identify since they may consist of one word showing strong feeling, *i.e.* ouch! wow! hurrah! Within a pupil product, there might well be a debate on, "Should a modifier be placed in the sentence to make meanings with greater clarity?" This might be an adjective or adverb as single words, phrases, or clauses. Grammar should make writings more precise and meaningful, with critical and creative thinking involved, as well as excitement. The writer experienced labeling words with different parts of speech, frequently, in the public school setting.

- should pupils experience placing one line under the subject, and two under the verb (predicate) when analyzing chosen sentences? A good discussion may be inherent in this activity. All scoldings and satire should be eliminated in teaching pupils. Each response must be accepted with diagnosis involved. Respecting learners is a part of the equation in good teaching. This activity is traditional, but it implies that pupils can be aided in writing by having a subject and predicate in a sentence.
- when *readiness* exists, should pupils experience diagramming sentences, in a sequential pattern throughout the grades? There is much involved here from the past where in the writers public school years, much attention was given to diagramming sentences. There can be considerable thought involved in placing words in diagram (See Bartini, 2008).

Colleagues of the writer on the university level believe that solid, demanding courses in grammar assists in pupils doing quality written work. Others are not so sure on this point of view. Whatever beliefs are held, learning activities in grammar should be meaningful, interesting to secure learner attention, purposeful, and sequentially presented. Above all, relevancy is very salient in the cognitive and affective domains when grammatical skills obtained are put to use in written work (See Steele, 2010).

Conclusion

Grammar can be taught well by using psychological tenets whereby interest, meaning, purpose, and relevancy is involved. However, computers and innovative technology must also be encouraged and used. Harmony between the two are necessary (See Levine, 2011).

REFERENCES

Bartini, Maria (2008), "An Empirical Comparison of Traditional and Web-enhanced Classroom," *Journal of Instructional Psychology*, 35 (1), 3-12.

Ediger,Marlow (2011), "Shared Reading, The Pupil, and The Teacher," *Reading Improvement*, 48 (2), 55-58.

Ediger, Marlow, and D. Bhaskara Rao (2005), *Language Arts Curriculum*. New Delhi, India: Discovery Publishing House.

Kanti, K.S. (2011), A Study of Values of Prospective Secondary School Teachers in Relationship to Teacher Attitude and Teacher Aptitude. *Ph D Thesis in Education*, Acharya Nagarjuna University, Nagarjuna Nagar, A.P., India.

Levine, Arthur (2010), "Teacher Education Must Respond to Changes in America," Phi Delta Kappan, 92 (2), 19-24.

Steele, Carole Frederick (2011), "Inspired Responses," *Educational Leadership*, 68 (4), 64-69.

Tiedt, Iris M. (1982), *The Language Arts Handbook*. Englewood Cliffs, New Jersey: Prentice Hall, Inc.

Leadership in the Science Curriculum

Leadership is needed to improve any curriculum area, science included. Here, leaders may come from within the local public school teachers of science. A leader may be designated or a cooperative type of leadership might well emerge. The point being that science teachers must study, evaluate, and modify, if needed, current procedures of instruction. A quality science teacher's library should be available with the latest science teacher's journals as well as textbooks and audio-visual aids, to invigorate the teaching of science. Science teachers need to read subject matter and discuss related ideas among participants. Relevant ideas must be tried out in the classroom with results of teaching reported to the inservice deduction group. Leadership, then, may focus on the following inservice activities:

- reading and discussing selected ideas from science teaching journals and textbooks;
- encouraging members to incorporate in teaching that which meets desired criteria;

- reporting to the group how the innovation worked out in the classroom;
- video-tape the new approach for purposes of analyzing by the inservice group (Ediger 2003).

Curriculum Development in Science

There are a plethora of additional means of improving science instruction. Growth in science teaching should be ongoing. The inservice group of science teachers must set up a schedule of times for meeting. The topics may be established ahead of time or be open ended, depending upon feelings of participants. The needs of teachers is highly salient. When supervising university student teachers, the writer noticed three important items in conducting an experiment. *First*, pupils could not see clearly what was transpiring. Thus, selected pupils could not observe the experiment carefully due to seating arrangements or the materials used were not large enough. *Second*, pupils jumped to hasty conclusions without observing what truly did occur in the experiment, based on evidence. *Third*, there were too many variables in an experiment without holding all variables constant, except the one being tested. Objectivity in clarity of thinking is very important in science. Pupils with teacher guidance need to discuss the results of the experiment which involves critical and creative thinking, as well as problem solving. With inservice education, science experiments need to be carefully chosen and relevant to pupils. Inservice education may improve experimentation as a learning activity in ongoing lessons and units of study (See Mechta 2010).

Science experiments may be used to initiate, develop, as well as culminate a unit of study. To extend learnings, pupils might well read from a reputable source of information. Depending upon where pupils are in reading achievement and the kind of reference source used, learners may need assistance in the following:

- *word recognition*. Unknown words may be pronounced by the teacher or a capable reader. Better yet, to have pupils become independent in reading science materials, a pupil may need help with context clues. This approach assists pupils to think of a word which fits in meaningfully with the rest of the sentence or paragraph. Context clues also guide pupils in vocabulary development since the surrounding words will help to ascertain a working definition. Unknown words may be posted on a word wall whereby learners may later rehearse the identification and meaning of these words.

- *background information*. Learning is based upon what had been acquired previously; the content might be hazy and lack clarity which good teaching may overcome.
- if basal textbooks are utilized, the new words may be seen in print on a whiteboard prior to reading subject matter. These words may be discussed so that understanding of content is involved. From discussions related to the illustrations in the basal or brought in by the teacher, problems or questions may be identified for which solutions may be found through the actual reading experience. Extended learnings are also invited whereby pupils with teacher guidance identify a problem, gather information from a variety of reference sources, develop an hypothesis, test the hypothesis, and revise it if need be with critical and creative thinking (See Dryfoos 2008).

A project method may also be used to encourage pupil interest. The project might well involve a construction activity. Here, pupils with teacher guidance in an ongoing science unit may decide upon a model to be made. There are myriad models which may be constructed. Thus, pupils might be curious about developing a solar collector. Once the purpose is established, then plans must be made for its fruition. Information from a variety of reference sources need to be gathered including the internet and computer sources. Relevant information must be acquired to fulfill the purpose. Evaluation of what is salient needs to be sorted from that which lacks saliency. Thus, much content might well be acquired, but what is relevant needs to be selected. After the planning has been completed, then the actual execution of these need to be incorporated as learning experiences. These learning activities need to emphasize completeness, neatness, and conscientious work (See Darling-Hammond 1998).

Committee work may be stressed in developing the project. Criteria for doing quality small grow endeavors need to be stressed. Thus, the following are significant:

- each participate optimally, but no one dominating the committee
- members working for the good of developing a quality project
- individuals not participating wholeheartedly need encouragement and motivation to achieve. Each member of the committee is appraised in terms of effort put forth
- good human relations is emphasized in the learning experience; quality attitudes are of utmost importance (National Research Council, 2001).

Library Books to Expand Science Learnings

Science library books need to be ample in number for each unit of study. They need to be on diverse categories such as those dealing with biology, chemistry, earth science, and the environment. Pupils with teacher guidance might then select sequential books on their reading levels. With scaffolding of ideas contained in library books, the science teacher might well assist pupils to achieve at a hinger level than would ordinarily be the case. Challenge and positive achievement are two major concepts to emphasize in teaching and learning situations (See Pearman, 2008).

The contents of each library book may be used in discussions as these related science units are taught. Enjoyment in reading science materials also must be in the offing. This becomes a motivator for increased learner achievement. In addition to using library book content in discussions, they might well be also utilized in the following ways:

- in sustained silent reading (SSR) whereby special time is devoted to choice of reading materials for pupils to read silently to themselves
- in individualized reading in which the self selected reading material is discussed with the teacher at the end of that selection. The teacher may notice pupil comprehension and understanding of science subject matter as well as oral reading skills
- in the teacher reading orally to pupils during story hour
- in peer discussion groups whereby participants assist each other with scaffolding of ideas (Ediger 2007).

Skills for Science Teachers and Inservice Education to become proficient participants within the framework of inservice education, science teachers need to collaborate. This involves cooperation, acceptance, and harmonious relationships. Trust must be developed among participants to work toward the goal of improving the curriculum. Collaboration involves dialogue. Dialogue emphasizes communicating with each other with clarity, meaning, and respect. Rudeness and intimidation have no roles to play in furthering the presenting of ideas relevant to the improvement of teaching and learning situations. There are a plethora of inservice education situations whereby collaboration and dialogue are needed as in the following:

- constructivism *versus* behaviourism;
- small group endeavours *versus* individual activities;
- cooperation *versus* competition;
- depth *versus* breadth in ongoing science lessons and units of study;
- locally selected objectives *versus* mandated objectives;
- portfolios *versus* testing to ascertain learner achievement and progress (See Tompkins 2006).

Each of the above asterisked items needs thorough discussion in order to facilitate modifying science instruction where necessary. The focal point must be upon the learner in determining what is best.

REFERENCES

Darling-Hammond, L (1998), "Teachers and Teaching," *Educational Researcher*, 27(1), 5-15.

Dryfoos, Joy G. (2008), "Centers of Hope," *Educational Leadership*, 65 (7), 38-43.

Ediger, Marlow and D. Bhaskara Rao (2002), *Teaching Science Successfully*. New Delhi, India: Discovery Publishing House, Chapter Six.

Ediger, Marlow and D. Bhaskara Rao (2007), *Schol Science Education*. New Delhi, India: Discover Publishing House.

Mechta, Meenakshi (2010), "Personality Needs and Academic Achievement of Sr. Secondary Students," *Edutracks*, 8 (7), 27-30. Printed in India.

National Research Council (2001), *National Science Education Standards for Schools*, Washington, DC: National Science Teachers Association.

Pearman, Cathy 2008), *"Independent Reading of CD-ROM Storybooks,"* 61 (8), 594-603.

Tompkins, G. E. (2006), *Literacy for the 21st Century: A Balanced Approach*. Upper Saddle River, New Jersey: Pearson Prentice Hall.

Revisiting the Concepts of Scope and Sequence in Science

Two highly valuable concepts to consider in science instruction are scope (what should be taught) and sequence (when should these be brought into teaching and learning situations). Science lesson plans and units of study must reflect the saliency of these two concepts.

Scope in Science Teaching

The objectives of instruction will indicate the totality of science subject matter and skills to be taught. There is much to incorporate in any unit of study. Thus, the scope must receive careful consideration in terms of that which is relevant. Which understandings and abilities should the science teacher emphasize, for example, in a unit on "The Changing Surface of the Earth?" The science teacher, after much planning, might well consider content such as the following:

* active volcanos and how they make for changes in geology/geography;
* the formation of igneous, sedimentary, and metamorphic rocks;

* fossil information providing subject matter dealing with the history and evolution of the planet earth;
* mudslides, floods, erosion, tornados, hurricanes, among others (Ediger, 2007).

Each of the above asterisked items may be stated as a general objective or written in measurable terms. How will pupils achieve these objectives? Learning opportunities then must be chosen. Thus, a variety of experiences need provision to provide for different aptitudes, intelligences, and interest differences among learners. Concrete, semi-concrete, and abstract learning activities must be in the offing to meet pupil needs. They may be adapted to the following:

- individual and collective/committee endeavours;
- problem solving and project methods;
- construction experiences and audio-visual presentations;
- reading of abstract materials;
- written work including writing summaries, reports, conclusions, outlines, as well as narratives/information content;
- speaking experiences such as oral and book reports, dramatizations, discussions, peer group presentations, among others;
- listening activities in science units of study including power point presentations, DVDs, CDs, as well as those interacting with speaking experiences listed previously above;
- art, music, social studies, mathematics, and literature integration as they relate to ongoing lessons;
- quality feedback from testing situations (See National Research Council, 1996).

The breadth of objectives and experiences provide for scope in the science curriculum. Learning may be maximized in science for pupils by paying careful attention to scope in science. Trivia and the unimportant are then weeded out.

Sequence in Science Learnings

Sequence is highly salient as a topic to discuss. The order of providing learning experiences makes for achievement or a lack thereof. Some guidance for the science teacher might come from a salient rule of starting with the concrete or life like experiences such as experiments in ongoing lessons and units of study. This is followed with the semi-concrete as in a power point presentation whereby pupils perceive illustrations, not reality, of what is being studied as in fish, amphibians, reptiles, birds, and mammals, in a science unit on animals. Rich discussions do occur from the concrete as well as the semi-concrete. These examples should provide needed background information to use in scaffolding in which pupils are ready to achieve higher cognitive level objectives with abstract leanings including reading of science subject matter in particular. The concrete, semi-concrete, and abstract might well include oral communication, listening, and writing skills, as well as related subject matter from other academic disciplines (See Eisner, 2006).

Instruction should always be adapted to the learner's present level of achievement. The writer is a firm believer in Vygotsky's Zone of Proximal Development in that encouragement and challenge are possible with good teaching for the learner to extend his/her repertoire of knowledge and skills. Inherent in this statement is the motivation factor whereby the following motivate (provide a higher energy level for learning):

- develop and maintain pupil interest in a topic our project. Interest is a powerful factor in learning and carries the study of a topic or a project to fruition;
- assist learners to see the relevance or usefulness of science subject matter being considered and studied;
- consider the developmental level of the pupil in the teaching and learning process; scaffold learning to guide learners to higher levels of progress;
- permit pupil input into learning activities and

opportunities whereby choices may be made in terms of what to learn;

- help pupils to achieve feelings of belonging; being an isolate violates learner feelings of adequacy;
- guide pupils to be successful achievers within the framework of a challenging science lesson or unit of study;
- meet esteem needs of individuals with honest praise for work well done. Each pupil craves recognition for improved performance (See National Science Teachers Association, 2001).

There are a plethora of instructional plans in aiding pupil science achievement. The following may be used entoto or in separate/integrated situations:

- personalizing instruction whereby the science teacher plans learning activities individually with pupils. The experiences are designed to meet personal needs in science instruction;
- learning centres in which pupils, individually, choose from alternative learning opportunities at different centres, each of which contains task cards for assistance in making selections;
- a basics approach whereby pupils are taught sequential learnings using a carefully chosen science textbook. Audio-visual aids, as well as other technology, are utilized to enrich pupil experiences;
- a science curriculum, heavily endowed with the latest in technology such as lap tops, cell phones, iPods, iTunes, science video games, smart phones, white boards, as well as other mobile technology. Technology might also be integrated with each of the above asterisked plans of instruction (Ediger, 2009).

Within each plan of instruction, pupils might well acquire increasingly complex science subject matter content. Thus, with quality sequence, optimal learner achievement is possible.

Conclusion

Science teachers and supervisors need to pay careful attention to the scope of the curriculum. This involves careful selection of what is taught to minimize the rival band the unimportant. Sequence, a related concept, stresses the science teacher ordering when subject matter is to be emphasized. Good, planned sequence with scaffolding assists pupils to achieve well with instruction related to the developmental levels of learners (See Brady, 2008).

REFERENCES

Brady, Marion (2008), "Cover the Material or Teach Students to Think?" *Educational Leadership*, 65 (5), 64-67.

Ediger, Marlowl and D. Bhaskara Rao (2007), *School Science Education*. New Delhi, India: Discovery Publishing House, Chapter Six,

Ediger, Marlow (2009), "Oral Communication and Science Teaching," *Experiments in Education*, 37(1), 17-20.

Eisner, Elliot (2006), "The Satisfaction of Teaching," *Educational Leadership*, 63 (6), 44-47.

National Research Council (1996), *National Science Education Standards*. Washington DC: National Science Teachers Association.

National Science Teachers Association (2001), *Classroom Assessment and the National Education Standards*. Washington DC: NSTA.

Self Efficacy and the Science Teacher

Self efficacy is an important concept for science teachers to emphasize. Science teachers need to grow in knowledge, skills, and attitudes. This growth is exemplified in teaching quality whereby pupils are the beneficiaries of instruction. The science teacher must achieve in the direction of assisting pupils to realize their individual potential.

Individuals live in a scientific world whereby pupils experience matter in its diverse forms and potentials. Everywhere one looks, hears, smells, tastes, and touches, the world of science is there. Measurement instruments extend these experiences. Thus, it behooves the teacher and pupils to be aware of the scientific world and extend curiosities, interests, and abilities in that direction. Scientific literacy then is becoming increasingly important with its many contributions to society.

Developing Self Efficacy

The science teacher has a plethora of pupils to provide for in teaching and learning situations. They are of diverse ability levels and from different socio-economic levels. The quality of experiences is different one from the other with some having travelled more extensively, visited numerous sites of interest, and have parents who provided for their physical safety, emotional, and esteem needs. The achievement levels in science differs also. Thus, the science teacher needs to become increasingly proficient in teaching pupils whose personalities and past experiences vary. He/she needs to grow in science achievement in terms of subject matter and methods of instruction so that each pupil may be assisted to attain more optimally. Self efficacy then becomes a major goal for the science teacher.

A professional library must be established in a selected room or area to assist science teachers to develop efficacy. Teachers then have numerous opportunities to keep up with the latest trends in teaching. Periodicals, textbooks containing useful subject matter for teaching pupils in diverse areas of science, science eduction textbooks which clearly describe quality methods of instruction, educational psychology texts, sociology/anthropology texts dealing with diverse cultures, among others. Science teachers need encouragement to pursue reading content of interest and purpose in teaching and learning.

Ample opportunities must be provided for teachers to observe other professionals in teaching science. Discussions should follow which enhance professionalism. Establishing purpose for learning, securing interests of pupils, and providing for the needs of each pupil are imperative. Units in science need to be developed with other science teachers. High quality objectives, learning activities to achieve these objectives, and evaluation procedures to notice if objectives have been attained are musts! By mastering elements of the science curricula, the teacher has more strategies in the repertoire for teaching pupils, thus increasing tenets of self efficacy in providing for individual differences. Success in teaching builds upon success in becoming efficacious.

Observing models of excellence in teaching science might well aid the teacher in doing what makes for quality instruction. The model, for example, may come from viewing video clips. A teaching team may analyze the contents and assist in applying what is agreed upon. These vicarious experiences need to be sought out which provide sources for emulation. There are good videos on inquiry learning, problem solving, the project method, among others.

Through conferences and social persuasion, the teacher might also improve instruction. A supervisor, team leader, or coach, strong in human relations and with a wealth of ideas for quality teaching can certainly be an asset to science teachers. They can offer ideas during an observational visit on specific approaches in teaching quality when analyzing instruction. The model presented needs to be such that the teacher accepts innovative subject matter and methodology in teaching. The teacher then wishes to emulate the model with content suggested by a science specialist.

Motivation comes from within the teacher who attempts to overcome complexities and difficulties. Rich past experiences, involving success, build up a reservoir of ideas and challenges which assist in overcoming that which initially might have been perceived as unavoidable. Self efficacy aids feelings of confidence and strength to resolve complex situations. The stronger the self efficacy feelings are, the better the attitudes are in perceived situations. Thus, the efficacious teacher is better able to cope with stressful and depressing situations. Even though challenges are invited, the efficacious science teacher realizes situations which provide difficulties in coping. He/she assesses what is challenging and needs resolutions *versus* those which possibly exceed talents and abilities possessed. The flexible dividing line here is open ended, but self evaluation provides possible limits. Those who lack self efficacy shy away from difficult tasks. They tend not to be interested in doing what is complex and yet might be achievable with effort. The power of self efficacy in science is in evidence from the following:

* the level of attainment in an ongoing setting
* the learning activity being involved with

* effort put forth in an experience
* choices made in a learning experience
* persistence in the completion of an activity.

Contrast the above asterisked items with those having low efficacy. Low efficacy stresses ineffective goal setting. These individuals do poorly on tasks to be completed. They choose to work on easier tasks with less effort put forth. These learning activities are less complex to complete. Putting forth as little effort as possible, these pupils may be classified as being 'lazy.' A low level of motivation is in evidence. Inward motivation of pupils is necessary in these cases and situations as well as scaffolding. The science teacher must have a wide range of teaching skills and methodologies available here.

Teaching for Optimal Learner Achievement

The science teacher may secure and develop excellent guidelines to assist pupil progress. Self efficacy is a goal to attain for pupils, as well as teachers. To start with, the teacher needs to ascertain where each learner is prior to teaching a lesson/unit of study. He/she will increasingly become familiar where each pupil is at the starting point. This occurs with rich experiences in teaching and learning situations. First of all then, the science teacher needs to begin a learning activity with where the pupil is presently in achievement, as well as relate this to the chosen objectives of instruction. As much as possible, this should harmonize with the learning styles of pupils. Styles of learning include working collaboratively *versus* achieving by the self, deductive as compared to inductive procedures, an explanations approach *versus* discovery learning, problem solving, as well as project methods of instruction.

In going from the known to the unknown in subject matter and skills learning helps pupils to be successful learners. To completely avoid determining where each pupil is presently in achievement prior to teaching, will minimize pupil efforts due to selected pupils having already having mastered what is taught or it being too complex to attain. There still will be individual differences to provide for and the science teacher may scaffold for those needing additional assistance in learning. Assisting pupils, here, to notice that which needs more attention in learning brings improved order to the teaching/learning situation. Helping pupils to reflect upon past learnings will guide individuals to ascertain what is/is not understood.

Once past achievement is known so that new learnings may be built upon what was previously achieved, the science teacher is ready to introduce new subject matter and skills. There are numerous methods to be used to help pupils attain objectives of instruction including the use of abstract, semi-concrete, and concrete materials of instruction. Seamless learning in use of these materials makes for quality sequence whereby continuous achievement is possible. Meaning needs to be attached to each fact, concept, and generalization acquired. Thus, pupils understand what is taught; content and skills are not memorized for testing purposes, but are used in discussions, committee work, as well as in every day tasks in school and in society. Relevant scientific knowledge is then in the offing. Relevancy pertains to important ideas, useful in school and in society. Meaningful learnings then accrue with quality sequence. Inservice education for science teachers should include proper sequencing of subject matter and skills so that new learnings are built, rather continuously, upon what is known.

Evaluation of pupil progress must be ongoing. Teacher observation in the classroom stresses the teacher providing assistance as necessary when help is needed in point and time. Teacher observation must use updated criteria in the assessment process to aid optimal learner progress. Politely, assistance must be provided when utilizing teacher observation to appraise learner performance. Teacher written tests which possess high validity and reliability might also be used to ascertain what pupils have learned, including multiple choice, true/false, and essay test items. Feedback is then provided to the science teacher in terms of what must be retaught. This should help in providing pupils with better sequence in learning. Success in teaching is salient when self efficacy is being stressed. Successful teaching experiences builds confidence within the teacher in meeting needs of pupils. Regardless of the category of the pupil be it gifted, talented, average in achievement, slow learner, mentally/physically handicapped, among others, the efficacious teacher is able to provide for individual differences and assist each to attain as much as possible.

Different Philosophies of Teaching and Learning

The flexible efficacious teacher of science is able to do well under diverse philosophies of instruction. Behaviourism, as one school of thought, stresses the salience of teaching for ends or the measurably stated objectives of instruction. These objectives have little or no leeway in interpretation, be they school wide or stated mandated. The learning activities, chosen by the science teacher, guide pupils to attain the sequential, highly specific objectives. Sequence here resides in the teacher teaching for pupils to achieve each end, or those who selected the mandated objectives. Standardized tests are utilized to measure pupil attainment, generally once a year. Pupils, too, are promoted if each test is passed in grades three through eight. Then, too, an exit test must be passed by secondary students for graduation with a diploma. In addition, the school or school system must pass Adequate Yearly Progress (AYP), each school year until 2014 when the level of competency is reached. Each school year, the yearly test becomes more complex, even though as school district failed to meet AYP standards. The AYP test has frustrated many schools in meeting its standards, perhaps as many as eighty per cent of schools have failed AYP.

Somewhat opposite of behaviourism is constructivism. Constructivism greatly minimizes testing procedures to notice pupil achievement and progress. Rather, the pupils is the focal point of achievement, not attaining the measurably stated objectives which, of course, are not in evidence. They sequence their own learnings in science. Thus, as a science lesson/unit of study moves forward, the science teacher assists pupils to identify problems or broad questions. The problem is delimited in a discussion and subject to evaluation, resulting in an hypothesis. A science experiment is developed by pupils to secure information. The experiment evaluates the one variable and is carefully controlled, resulting in an answer. The answer may then be accepted, modified, or refuted. Pupils are heavily involved during the entire experiment. They identify the problem, locate information, do the experiment, and evaluate the hypothesis, among other necessities. The science teacher is a guide, a facilitator, and a resource person who encourages and assists learners to attain their goals.

Thus, the efficacious is competent and flexible to adapt to diverse strategies of teaching science.

16

Teaching the Social Studies and Emotional Intelligence

Social studies teaching involves not only knowledge and skills of the social sciences but also methodology of orderly strategies to utilize in the instructional arena. Each pupil needs to attain optimally in those academic disciplines making up the social studies, namely history, geography, political science, anthropology/sociology with emphasis upon culture, and economics. At the same time, quality human relations must exist in working with other teachers, the school administrator, and pupils. This brings to the attention of emotional intelligence (El) in teaching and learning situations (Ediger and Rao, 2007).

Emotional Intelligence and Teaching the Social Studies Keeping emotions under control is a vital consideration in working with others (Nazareth, 2010). What has been said in anger is regretted and it becomes difficult to regain confidence in these situations. Thus, it behooves teachers to be aware of one's own emotions. Self awareness is very important here in regulating one's own behaviour. The social studies teacher, in providing for individual differences, needs to be proficient in working with individuals, small groups, and large group instruction. When having pupils move from a large group to committee endeavours, this needs to be done seamlessly to avoid distractions and unnecessary noises. The goals of instruction must be focussed upon at all times, involving structural ideas from the academic disciplines in unit teachings well as quality human relations.

The social studies teacher must reflect upon successes to develop well in emotional intelligence; he/she needs to learn from failures but not have these overtake the teacher or hinder instruction. Success builds upon success when the teacher is well prepared for each day of instruction and utilizes methodology which assists pupils to attain sequentially in ongoing lessons and units of study. Learner progress and achievement is of utmost important. Faith in the self as a social studies teacher builds confidence in making quality decisions in the classroom. The teacher then leans upon the self for high quality decisions to be made. If he/she falters in decision making, then there are weaknesses in choices made. It is salient to possess an adequate self concept within the framework of emotional intelligence. There must be a quality self concept in decision making and for pupils to emulate this role model (Goleman, 1998).

It is salient for the social studies teacher to accept responsibility for outcomes which accrue in teaching; blaming others rarely helps the teacher to become a responsible person. To improve teaching quality, the social studies teacher must grow in knowledge and skills which can be attained in a variety ways:

- read, study, and implement significant content from the social sciences, as well as methods of teaching the social studies;
- attend and actively participate in state and national conferences such as the local state and the National Council for the Social Studies, among others;
- observe and consult with outstanding teachers in diverse facets of social studies instruction;

- be a leader in participating in local departmental meetings in the social studies;
- emphasize the salience of attending workshops in teaching the social studies;
- work together with other teachers on harmonizing issues (Ediger, 2010).

Coping with difficulties is a must and needs to be worked out satisfactorily (Goleman, 1996). For instance, there are a plethora of interpretations in history, in particular, which may bring in the wrath of parents such as those of the fundamentalist right wing versus those adhering to a liberal point of view. Unfortunately, it is difficult, at times, in having the right wing *versus* the liberals' view other beliefs as well as selected philosophies of life. The teacher cannot gloss over these discrepancies, but must face them squarely in discussions, debates, and question/answer times. Persistence is a key quality here with confidence in the self. Focussing upon success rather than failure helps teachers to persist.The teacher needs to adapt and learn coping skills, outside the classroom, such as the following:

- walking briskly at suitable times
- having a humourous conversation with a colleague
- confide concerns with a trustworthy teacher
- think of alternative ways of presenting controversial subject matter
- voice concerns to the school supervisor or principal.

The social studies teacher must show respect for the thinking of others, paying attention also to non-verbal communication. Rudeness and unkind remarks need to be analyzed and modified. People are different from each other in a plethora of ways and this must be accepted; each person should have the right to express adhered to beliefs honestly. He/she possesses feelings, values, and ideals about current events and happenings. Self control is of utmost importance when listening to the thinking and feelings of others. These thoughts and feelings might irritate selected persons, but, and if responding, rational ideas must prevail. It must be accepted that disagreeable ideas can be tolerated without nasty comments being made.

Motivation to achieve comes from within, not from external rewards. Highly motivated social studies teachers are passionate about their teaching and find rewards from within the instructional arena. Their success comes, in part, from recognizing emotions in others. Possessing empathy indicates maturity. A school is a social institution with people of a variety of cultures and needs.

A Teacher Centred Classroom

A teacher centered approach to teaching may be at opposite ends of the continuum with that of El. A teacher centred classroom might well focus upon a strict regimen the school environment. The following might will be observed:

- pupils seated in neat rows with carefully chosen textbooks, workbooks, and work sheets providing the majority of instructional materials;
- each pupil completes his/her own assigned lessons with very minimal small group work;
- the teacher observes that each pupil completes work on time; assistance is immediately provided for those who goof off. Orderly, quiet classrooms are vital to avoid distractions;
- completed lessons are checked by the teacher and incorrect answers must be corrected. Pupils ask few questions unless it pertains directly to the problem(s) at hand;
- methods of instruction include lecture in large group sessions.

A set of teachers who used most of the above criteria in a write-up of actual teaching situations concluded the following:

We need to be cautious about adopting complicated, trendy, and expensive practices. We need to re-evaluate our affection for collaborative/cooperative learning, extensive technology, project based learning, and constructivism, as well as our disaffection for explicit direct instruction and strict discipline. These teachers were strict, direct, deeply committed, and respectful to students. Their students in turn respected them (Poplin, *et. al.*, 2011).

Conclusion

Individuals interact with others in social situations. Thus, the feelings of the self together with those of peers, adults, among others in society, need to be respected so that communication is genuine and thoughtful. When unkind situations evolve, communication becomes broken and it takes time to resurrect rational thinking. This is true in the social studies as well as other curriculum areas.

REFERENCES

Ediger, Marlow (2010), "Portfolios in the Social Studies," *College Student Journal*, 44 (4), 913-915.

Ediger, Marlow, and D. Bhaskara Rao (2007), *Teaching Social Studies*. New Delhi, India; Discovery Publishing House.

Goleman, Daniel (1996), *Emotional Intelligence*. New York; Bantam Books.

Goleman, Daniel (1998), *Working with Emotional Intelligence*. New York; Bantam Books.

Nazareth, Bruno (2010), Effect of Emotional Intelligence and Self Efficacy on B. Ed, Trainees on Their Academic Achievement. *Ph D Thesis*, Alaggappa University, Karaikudi, India.

Poplin, Mary, *et al.* (2011), "She is Strict for a Good Reason," Phi Delta Kappan, 92 (5), 39-43.

Developing Pupil Vocabularies in the Social Studies

A rich vocabulary is needed for pupil achievement in the social studies. There are new terms and words which pupils need to understand and use in ongoing units of study. They provide building blocks for ensuing lessons. Sequence is necessary in moving from the "known to the unknown" a phrase which Swiss educator Johann Friedrich Pestalozzi (1746-1827) made famous in his schools, especially when teaching the object lesson. Jumping too far ahead of pupil's present achievement levels makes for frustration whereas repeating and reviewing too frequently invites learner boredom and restlessness. Social studies teachers must ascertain where each pupil is presently in achievement before pursuing the new content. Individual differences need to be provided for as in vocabulary development; each differs in past experiences, interests, purpose, as well as in motivation (Ediger, 2011).

Involving Pupils in Vocabulary Development

There are a plethora of procedures in assisting pupils in vocabulary development. One approach pertains to pupils acquiring information from an adopted social studies textbook. If a pupil does not know the identification of a word, he/she may use context clues and fill in with a word, in place of the unknown, which harmonizes with the rest of the sentence or paragraph to make for meaningful learning. This word will also tend to provide a clear definition in context. Extended vocabularies may be developed through the use of context clues, as well as assisting in word recognition.

Electronic books help pupils to identify and establish meaning of ensuing words. Thus, the pupil paces the book to enjoy and comprehend reading of ideas. The words may be pronounced aloud as the content is pursued. If, for example, a child does not know the identification of a word encountered, he/she may follow along with the spoken voice. To ascertain the meaning of an unknown word, the child may highlight it and view its definition and use in the dictionary part of the programme.

Also, when pupils choose sequential library books to read, which relate directly to the unit being taught, pupils see new words in print in a meaningful, contextual manner. This is a good approach to use in vocabulary achievement. Pupils select and read, silently, subject matter which is of personal interest and tends to be on their individual reading level. Assistance in word recognition may be provided by the teacher or a good reader in the classroom. Pupil ownership of sustained silent reading programmes is possible when he/she chooses what is to be read. Periodically, a conference may be held with the classroom teacher upon completion of reading the library book. Here, the learner might read a short selection aloud to evaluate growth in word identification as well as briefly discuss the contents with the teacher. Pupil interest in reading self selected content is needed so that optimal social studies knowledge and vocabulary skills may be secured (Ediger, 2011).

During discussions of content read by pupils, they will acquire new vocabulary terms as a result. Extension of meanings accrue when subject matter is appraised; critical and creative thinking must be involved together with problem solving. Here, pupils review and rehearse vocabulary words. These may come from various social studies magazines and materials. Before pupils read a selection from the text, they should see the new words in print on a whiteboard. These words should be pronounced correctly by learners and used in a sentence to promote meaning. Pupils should also develop readiness by viewing the illustrations in the text. Johann Friedrich Herbart (1776-1841), an early advocate of the readiness concept when in lesson planning, he emphasized the following sequential steps: preparation (building background information), presentation of ensuing subject matter, association by relating new content with that previously presented, generalization in achieving broad ideas from the associations made, and use whereby pupils make some application of what has been learned. Each of these steps might well emphasize bringing in new vocabulary.

Too frequently, pupils do not look at the pictures to provide background information in reading social studies content as well as in aiding vocabulary development. As these activities proceed, learners will also raise questions which might well be recorded on the white board and answers discussed after reading the selection directly related to the ongoing unit of study. Rereading of subject matter might well be involved when debating answers to questions (See Stahl and Bravo, 2010).

Pupils should be encouraged to maintain vocabulary notebooks during a discussion. For instance in a unit on the Middle Ages, pupils may record concepts such as the following: apprentice, journey man, master, guilds, as well as regulation of products quality and equitable wages. Important vocabulary words should be printed neatly on a word wall in the classroom. The author in supervising university student teachers in the public schools has found that a word wall is an invaluable device for students, in their spare time, to look at, and review salient words previously encountered. When viewing these words, pupils discuss correct identification of each.as well as their inherent meanings. The social studies teacher must emphasize word study and their meanings as an important objective in each curriculum area. Too frequently, pupils experience a lack of success in reading social studies content, as well as reading across the curriculum, due to inadequately developed vocabularies (Praveena and Srinivasa, 2011).

A project method of teaching works well in the social studies. A hands on approach in learning is being emphasized here. A chosen project must extend learnings from what is being studied. Four to five pupils might work on a chosen project in which vocabulary development will be inherent. New terms will be mentioned in discussing how to proceed once the project is chosen. A project method will also add vocabulary to a pupil's repertoire as the subject matter related to the project is discussed collaboratively. Thus, in a unit of study on The Middle Ages, pupils will learn indepth vocabulary such as manor, cottages, castle, moat, serfs, blacksmith shop, mill to grind grain, lord and lady in a castle. These terms might well become meaningful in context in ensuing experiences pertaining to making a model of a manor. Pupils, in committees of three to four, construct each part of the model, using a variety of materials. Careful planning, and neat construction products are musts! Evaluation should be done in terms of planned criteria. These standards also provide guidance in terms of what is expected of learners in the ongoing experience. Rich learning activities, such as these, assist pupils to gain in vocabulary development. Then too, project methods aid pupils who prefer a hands on style of learning. Generally, most pupils enjoy a change of activities in ongoing units of study. Constructivism, as a psychology/ philosophy of learning, stresses that pupils sequence their own activities within a flexible framework. This is different from behaviourism in which pupils are taught to achieve measurably stated objectives of instruction, selected prior to instruction (See Woolfolk, 2004).

Another approach to emphasize in using AV aids is the implementation of power point presentations. Here, pupils view ordered slides on vital concepts. For example, in continuing the social studies unit on the Middle Ages, pupils might view the following: a squire, a knight, lance, spear, armour, shield, tournament, and horsemanship. Thus, pupils may learn about stages in becoming a knight as well as weapons used in their duties and responsibilities. A poster may be made showing pictorially the meaning of each concept and vocabulary term.

Conclusion

There are a plethora of rich experiences to aid pupil vocabulary development in the social studies. In addition to those indicated above, pupils with teacher assistance may engage in the following:

- doing research from computer information in providing an oral report on city / village life during the Middle Ages. These may be given individually or collaboratively;
- developing a mural integrating different facets of mediaeval life;
- dramatizing the role of a peasant/serf on a manor or a merchant in a trade fair;
- creating individual illustrations of a church on a manor, a mediaeval priest, manorial cottages, and an enclosed wall around a village;
- making a collage of diverse mediaeval sights and scenes;
- planning and doing a reader's theatre presentation. Learners from other classrooms my be invited to observe this activity.

Rich learning experiences in a multimedia approach help to guide optimal progress among learners. They assist pupil interest, motivation, and purpose in ensuing experiences involving social studies vocabulary development.

REFERENCES

Ediger, Mariow (2011), "Shared Reading: The Pupil, and the Teacher," *Reading Improvement*, 48 (2), 55-58.

Ediger, Mariow (2011), "Leadership in the Social Studies Curriculum," *Education*, 131 (4), 711-714.

Praveena, K.B., and K.S. Srinvasa, (2011), Interactive Multimedia: A Technology Wave in Education, "*Edutracks*, 10 (11), 6-8. Printed in India.

Stahl, Katherine A. Daugherty, and Marco A. Bravo (2010), "Contemporary Classroom Vocabulary Assessment for Content Areas," *The Reading Teacher*, 63 (7), 566-579.

Woolfolk, A. (2004), *Educational Psychology*, Ninth Edition. Boston, MA: Pearson.

18

Vocabulary Development in the Social Studies

Social studies vocabulary must receive high priority in teaching and learning situations. A meaningful vocabulary assists pupils to do well in listening, speaking, reading, and writing in ongoing lessons and units of study. A variety of methods and procedures need to be used to guide more optimal attainment. Pupils differ from each other in the level of vocabulary growth and these differences need to have prime consideration in the learning process. Objectives need incorporation which stress word meanings, and concepts which are salient should become an important part of the child's repertoire. The social studies teacher needs to evaluate which terms are poignant in the curriculum and incorporate these into relevant subject matter for pupil achievement.

Pupils tend to like to play with words which are relevant and useful in school and in society. They are increasingly able to communicate more effectively with others when variety and diversity of vocabulary terms are used more precisely. Vagueness in communication occurs when clarity in intended meanings are not in evidence. Sometimes words are not used correctly in context making for misunderstandings in human relations. Thus, social studies teachers need to identify vital words and phrases to emphasize when instructional procedures are developed and implemented (Ediger, 2010).

Vocabulary Development

Various ways will be discussed pertaining to helping pupils enrich their listening, speaking, reading, and writing vocabularies in the social studies. When reading from the basal textbook, learners should see new words in print, prior to reading its content. Learner attention must be focussed on these words on the whiteboard. A meaningful discussion should focus upon the context within which each word will be used. Background information is then provided in word recognition as well as in vocabulary development with pupils then possessing readiness factors for reading. They also need to discuss with teacher guidance illustrations in the text which might well illuminate meanings of these new vocabulary terms. There are additional ways in which pupils reinforce attached meanings such as when actually reading from the basal as well as discussing main and subordinate ideas read. The new vocabulary terms may be printed on the word wall in the classroom.

A second procedure in aiding pupil vocabulary growth emphasizes the social studies teacher using new concepts in discussions. There are a plethora of vocabulary terms which may come from different social science disciplines which provide subject matter for the social studies. These may include the following used in context as well as added to the word wall when stressed:

- economic concepts such as consumption of goods and services. Pupils may look around the classroom and school setting to notice inherent meanings. Thus, pupils may notice items of clothing purchased, as well as school supplies consisting of paper, pen/pencils, among others. Gross national product, production and distribution are additional valuable economic concepts;

- anthropological/sociological concepts including culture, language, artifacts, socio-economic levels, and other related concepts.

The above named academic disciplines may be expanded to include the following within ongoing social studies units:

- historical concepts such as duration in time, World War One, the Great Depression, World War Two, recessions, oil spills, off shore drilling, global warming, etcetera;
- geographical concepts—latitude, longitude, meridians, parallels, plains, plateaus, and polar regions;
- political science concepts such as federal, state, and local governments, as well as the United Nations. Socialism, democracy, communism, and totalitarian are additional salient political science concepts (See Parker, 2001).

A quality current events programme keeps the social studies curriculum updated. A rich vocabulary is then embedded. A pupil centred curriculum needs to be emphasized in that learners must understand what is taught and its relevancy. With relevancy, use is made of subject matter acquired. Content then is not taught and learned for its own sake, but it has utilitarian values in school and in society. Developmentally and age appropriate learnings must be provide with the style of learning preferred by the pupil. The style of learning might well stress constructivism with sequence determined largely by the pupil with teacher guidance, or deductively presented by the teacher in meaningful ways. A challenging curriculum may be in the offing through scaffolding or the vocabulary terms may need to be made concrete through understandable meanings.

Acceptable criteria for selecting vocabulary terms must be followed by the social studies teacher and might well involve the following:

- high expectations exist and yet the vocabulary encountered is achievable in meaning;

- success in vocabulary learning for each pupil is paramount within the framework of being understandable;
- indepth learnings involving quality sequence needs to be in the offing;
- positive interactions in the classroom eliminates rudeness and inconsiderate behavior in achieving positive attitudes;
- good citizenship behaviours integrate with purposeful vocabulary development activities (Ediger, 2010).

There are significant achievement levels in vocabulary development with, first of all, the pupil being able to recognize and pronounce the word correctly. This also has prerequisites such as using necessary phonetic principles as well as context clues when reading sentences and paragraphs. The pupil might then be able to define the vocabulary term and/or use it in a sentence. The recall level of cognition may be involved here. Next, the pupil is able to utilize the word in oral communication and written experiences. There needs to be planned experiences whereby the level of application is possible. This aids the learner to expand the use of these words and multiple meanings are attached. In the writer's experiences of supervising university student teachers, he has noticed pupils enjoying playing with words in providing a plethora of uses for each and possessing clarity within a contextual situation. Breadth of attached meanings for each vocabulary term indicates growth in learning as well as precision in usage. Flexibility in higher levels of thought makes it possible to be productive in usage of myriad vocabulary words in a variety of situations.

There are creative uses of newly acquired words which provide interesting learning opportunities. The writer noticed the development of acrostic poetry in a classroom which included new terms such as in the following ongoing unit of study:

producing food items for a supermarket
restocking the shelves for shoppers

ordering what is needed on the shoppers list
diligent workers keep shelves stocked
under careful supervision of the manager
canned goods are displayed attractively
the meat counter makes one hungry for steaks
in the midst of different kinds of bread
on the minds of consumers who do the shopping
no one complains about the distribution (See Tiedt, 1982).

A vocabulary concept, such as the above titled Production, may then be chosen for writing a creative poem. Acrostic poetry is relatively easy to write since it requires no rhyme, nor be of a specific length. It becomes difficult to determine words which rhyme as well as have a certain length. Pupils do need to see the acrostic in print which the social studies teacher needs to model. To initiate the individual writing of an acrostic, a group poem might be written with pupils brainstorming the title as well as sequential lines, with the teacher recording the ideas for all to see clearly The content clearly reflects pupil knowledge of production. A pupil's poem may become a part of his/her portfolio.

Evaluation of Achievement

A portfolio is a random selection of learner products. The latter does the selecting of entries with teacher guidance. Sequential progress might then be noticed in vocabulary growth as well as other facets of social studies achievement. Although test scores may be included in the portfolio, the entries therein provide direct evidence of pupil achievement in vocabulary development as well as progress made in ongoing units of study. Thus, the following, among others, may be included:

- written summaries, outlines, diary/log entries, and poems;
- recordings of oral book reports, committee endeavours, and dramatizations related to ongoing lessons in social studies;

- drawings, diagrams, charts, graphs, and other forms of statistical information;
- digital photos of products and processes studied within a unit of study (Ediger, 2007).

The portfolio provides excellent content for parent/teacher conferences whereby parents can discuss present levels of pupil achievement and what needs further emphasis. Test results may be included such as standardized tests. However, the following limitations need to be kept in mind when viewing test scores:

- multiple choice test items generally prevail which limits pupils to select from among four options with no opportunities to vary words used in personal, contextual written experiences;
- pupils, individually, are compared with each other in vocabulary progress and not in growth from past achievement;
- the finer nuances are not noted in test results such as the ability to use contextually acquired vocabulary in new situations;
- personal definitions are not listed, generally, in choosing a correct response from the multiple choice form;
- pupils may not have had opportunities to learn meanings related to the correct response in a multiple choice test item;
- validity is always a problem in that selected test items have not been aligned with the local curriculum (See Guilfoyle, 2006).

Conclusion

Vocabulary achievement is a highly salient factor in understanding subject matter in different academic disciplines; it is poignant for the pupil presently in the social studies and for future achievement in academia. Some will continue with technical education and all will eventually need to be knowledgeable in social studies content as a member in society. An informed citizenry is highly important.

REFERENCES

Ediger, Marlow (2010), "Constructivism and the Social Studies," *Edutracks*, 9 (7),13-14.

Ediger, Marlow (2010), *Effective School Curriculum*. New Delhi, India: Discovery Publishing House.

Ediger, Marlow (2007), "Balance in the Curriculum," *The Elementary Principal*, 20 (4), 7-8.

Guifoyle, Christy (2006), "NCLB: Is There Life Beyond Testing?" *Educational Leadership*, 64 (3), 8-13.

National Council for the Social Studies (1997), *Curriculum Standards for the Social Studies*. Edison, New York: Whitehurst and Clark.

Parker, Walter C. (2001), Social Studies in Elementary Education. Upper Saddle River, New Jersey: Prentice Hall, Inc.

Tiedt, Iris M. (1982), The Language Arts Handbook. Englewood Cliffs, New Jersey: Prentice Hall, Inc.

19

Collaboration in Teaching the Social Studies

Much is written about the need for collaboration in developing the social studies curriculum. Teachers need to work together harmoniously in selecting the best objectives, learning opportunities, and appraisal procedures. Too frequently, the same design is used over and over again without critically evaluating the social studies programme. With collaborative endeavours, each social studies teacher may benefit from interacting with others in curricular endeavours. What might be accomplished in working together?

Collaboration in the Social Studies

Together, teachers may plan and work collectively on devising a quality social studies curriculum. The objectives section might well be a starting point. Critical and creative thinking by teachers is necessary to solve relevant problems. The objectives section needs to be evaluated in terms of the following:

- do they emphasize subject matter which is salient and significant? Trivia and the unimportant may thus be weeded out;

- are vital facts, concepts, and generalizations organized sequentially?
- is subject matter integrated with other academic disciplines when it is relevant to do so?
- does the scope clearly indicate the breadth of content to be studied by leaners?
- are the objectives stated as precisely as possible so that pupil achievement may be evaluated in terms of these chosen ends of instruction?
- is there a balance between subject matter and skills objectives?
- are attitudinal objectives stressed adequately?

It is complex to determine answers to each of the above; however, adequate attention must be given to develop a quality social studies curriculum. With collaboration, participant social studies teachers analyze the present units of study being taught. There is then a renewed interest in subject matter, skills, and attitudes which comprise teaching and learning situations. Discussing each of these areas provide for growth and achievement among social studies teachers. Reflective thinking of one's own personal experiences in teaching also identifies problems and issues in curriculum development. New, agreed upon objectives need to be tried out in the classroom with results being reported back to the collaborative team members. After analysis, synthesis must be emphasized by combining results from analytic situations.

The learning opportunities, for collaborative study, may be combined with the objectives in teaching social studies. Learning opportunities are chosen to be aligned with the objectives. They need to be varied to provide for diverse levels of pupil achievement as well as different styles of learning. Pupils differ from each other in a plethora of ways and the needs of learners must be met with high quality, rich learning opportunities. The following need to be examined indepth, collaboratively by teachers of social studies, and solutions found pertaining to implementing quality learning opportunities for pupils:

- inductive *versus* deductive learning;
- large group, small groups, and individual study for pupils as compared to teaching the class as a whole;
- learning by discovery *versus* use of lecture/explanations in ongoing lessons and units of study;
- problem solving and project methods as compared to more traditional approaches of teaching;
- use of technology to upgrade the social studies curriculum as compared to a more heavy emphasis upon textbooks, workbooks, and work sheets.

Learning opportunities need to provide for individual differences. They also must be meaningful and make sense to the learner. Pupils need to be fully engaged and be assisted in developing interest in each lesson. It is also salient for learners to perceive purpose or reasons for learning. Objectives must reflect what is relevant in school and in society. Collaborative endeavours should assist teachers to become efficacious and confident in their ability to teach well. An adequate self concept is necessary for this to occur.

Appraisal techniques must be valid and reliable. They must measure if pupils have achieved vital objectives. The following evaluation procedures need to be used to ascertain if social studies objectives have been attained:

- teacher written tests to measure achievement in ongoing lessons and units of study
- these tests need to be formative to ascertain pupil progress within a unit of study as well as summative or end of unit tests. Benchmark tests might well determine if pupils have achieved selected goals at a particular time within a unit of study.
- mandated tests given annually to evaluate learner progress.
- teacher observation to detect misunderstandings and needed corrections made as a social studies lesson progresses.

- self evaluation by pupils in terms of desired criteria.

Collaborative endeavours can do much to improve all facets of teaching social studies, including the evaluation procedures. Self evaluation by teachers is important and answers to the following questions need to be pursued:

- do I reflect upon my teaching to notice what works and what needs to be improved upon?
- am I growing as a professional in teaching the social studies?
- will pupils be adequately prepared to live as citizens in a democracy?
- is there balance among the different social science disciplines which comprise the social studies?
- do learners experience a relevant curriculum?
- did social studies teachers work together harmoniously in collaborative endeavours?
- are pupil interests in social studies growing?
- do they ask stimulating questions?
- do learners perceive authentic purposes for teaching and learning situations?
- am I developing feelings of self efficacy?

When teachers work in collaborative situations, they need to have access to quality library materials. A special section of the school library needs to house social studies teaching journals, university textbooks in teaching the social studies, video-tapes showing classrooms in action, and recordings of teaching the social studies by professors from diverse universities.

Collaborative Approach in Teaching the Social Studies

Social studies teachers who have appraised the total curriculum may also volunteer to teach collaboratively. Collective decision making without a designated leader emphasizes the following:

- leadership emerges as ideas are expressed for daily lesson plans and units of instruction. Each participant becomes a leader as he/she presents ideas for objectives, learning opportunities, and appraisal procedures. In evaluating the worth of each, the total group is involved in planning.

- content for the discussion comes from personal experiences, research data, journal articles, and university teaching social studies textbooks, among others. Examining ideas involves critical thinking, creative thinking in coming up with new ideas, as well as problem solving.
- assessment of ideas are based in their individual worth for developing a worthwhile programme of social studies. The subject matter must be useful to pupils presently as well as in society, in developing citizens who work toward improving society.
- teachers, individually or collectively, may volunteer to teach the class as a whole. Strengths of teachers must be used here on a rotation basis. Small group instruction needs to follow and involves all social studies teachers who collaborated in curriculum development. Pupils also need to select and work on individual projects, supervised by these same teachers.
- evaluation of pupil progress must involve all members of the collaborative teaching approach. A variety of valid and reliable methods should be used. These include teacher observation, mandated testing results, standardized tests, and teacher written tests such as multiple choice, essay, and short answer. Results from pupil evaluation should feed instruction. Thus, social studies teachers must use evaluative findings to improve instruction such as in the following:

  (*a*) specific subject matter misunderstandings

  (*b*) skills missing in pupil's repertoire—reading information from different kinds of maps and globes, locating information from reference sources including the internet and world wide web, writing summaries and conclusions, active participation in discussions and oral communication activities, and reading for a variety of purposes.

(*c*) areas of critical and creative thinking and problem solving as well as metacognition which need more emphasis.

- resource personnel, such as university social science/social studies professors should also have ample input, when possible, in developing a viable curriculum. A series of meetings planned with these professors may well provide impetus, also, in working toward curriculum improvement.

Conclusion

Collaboration involves working together to develop a quality social studies curriculum. Designing lessons and units of study assists in determining scope and sequence in the social studies. Collaborative teaching further stresses the importance of using talents and skills of teachers. The following are benefits of working well with others in collaborative endeavours in the social studies:

- participants learn from each other to improve teaching quality;
- more than one mind is better than a single mind to determine relevance;
- teacher support is necessary to implement and appraise the social studies curriculum. Many knowledgeable persons should be involved in curriculum improvement, including school administrators, curriculum directors, and lay people/parents.

Social studies instruction is important for all since it involves developing a good citizen with all the necessary inherent qualities needed and being developed subsequently in ongoing lessons and units of study.

Metacognition, Reading and the Social Studies

A considerable amount of reading is generally emphasized in the social studies.This may cause problems, especially for those having difficulties in decoding. There is much the social studies teacher can do to assist pupils in reading comprehension. A repertoire of strategies need to be in the offing to aid pupils in developing meanings from print. Basal textbooks, accompanying workbooks, primary sources of information, the internet, among others, contain abstractions which need to be understandable in subject matter content. It is indeed frustrating for pupils to have reading assignments which lack meaning. Learners must be assisted to achieve as optimally as possible in all learning opportunities including reading in the social studies. What might be done to facilitate these kinds of activities?

Guidelines in Teaching

The teacher should always stress going from the known to the unknown in teaching/learning situations. Thus, illustrations, directly related to the lesson/unit being studied might well be utilized as a strategy in assisting pupils in reading. Each illustration needs elaboration which guides pupils to relate to the ensuing content. Pupils, also, need to predict what will transpire as a result of reading. Predictions may be recorded on the whiteboard; pupils may check to notice how closely the predictions came about. This assists pupils to focus upon the subject matter content. Subsequently, ideas obtained may be discussed and integrated with predictions made. Reflection is emphasized with recalling previous knowledge as well as with related predictions. This makes it possible, too, to come up with creative ideas. Novel, unique thoughts are then in the offing. Relationship of knowledge is salient to stress in securing background information, prior to the ensuing reading activity, with possibilities to think of what might happen as the experience progresses (Ediger, 2009).

Too frequently, pupils are not lead to reflect, thus making for shallowness in thinking. Indepth thought encourages, not only creative thinking, but also critical thought. The reader does not accept social studies content read as fact, but analyzes subject matter into component categories. This allows specifics to be separated in terms of absolutes from tentativeness, imagination from reality, as well as fiction from non-fiction. Subject matter then becomes more holistic when this separation and then integration has occurred. Ideas in the social studies are subject to change and are definitely not fixed and final (Ahmad, 2009). The inquiring mind perceives gaps in knowledge and seeks wholeness. Thus within the project method and unit of study, pupils with teacher guidance may decide, for example, upon a construction project related to a social studies unit on grain farming. This breathes reality and practicality into the social studies. Plans for the model need to be made including the following:

- crop rotation and possible terracing, *e.g.* wheat rotated with soybeans and terraces made on hilly land to minimize/avoid soil erosion
- storage bins on the farm to store grain, prior to its selling on the open market

- model self propelled combines and tractors with air conditioned cabs
- large trucks or an eighteen wheeler which hauls the grain from the combine to the metal storage bins on the farm
- grain augurs which augur the grain from the truck into the storage bin.

In metacognition, pupils develop and focus upon broad and supporting ideas such as, "Farming methods have changed much in the last twenty years to include self propelled combines which cut a forty foot wide swath in the wheat field at one time. All of the latest tractors and combines have air conditioned cabs. Farming is highly specialized with grain farms, dairy farms, cage layers for egg production, broilers (young chickens), or hog complexes. It is indeed rare for a farm to have more than one enterprise."

Metacognition then requires a large fund of developmentally appropriate knowledge to go from the known to the unknown when reading. The knowledge provides background information to make the ensuing familiar when reading. Vocabulary study is important and must be stressed prior to and during reading, silently or orally. These new words may be printed in neat manuscript letters on the white board for all too see clearly. They should be discussed in terms of meaning and used in sentences, related to those to be read. Pupils must be taught to reflect upon these learnings and raise questions pertaining to what is not understood (Ediger, 2009).

For needed word recognition techniques while reading, the pupil must reflect upon using context clues, phonics, as well as seeing smaller words within the larger word to make use of subject matter read. Dividing an unrecognized word into prefixes, suffixes, and root, also aids in reading holistically. He/she needs to attend to major generalizations and supporting details. This adds structure to main ideas acquired. Continually, the reader must pay attention to comprehension by reflecting upon what has been read. Retention, through reflection, is salient in reading (See Parsons, 2008)!

Follow-up Learning Opportunities

Follow-up experiences should be open-ended, but include evaluating each prediction prior to reading. These should be assessed in an atmosphere of respect. Ridicule, rudeness, and feelings of haughtiness have no role to play in a quality social studies programme. Developing good citizens becomes a major objective. Civility is often lacking in the media, in school, and in society, making it necessary for schools to modify and remediate these behaviours. Questions raised by pupils need exploration and answers found. Here, problem solving, as an extended learning activity, becomes important. Thus, a relevant problem by pupils is identified within an ongoing unit of study. The problem needs to be delimited so that it is capable of being solved. An hypothesis is developed with a variety of reference sources used to secure necessary information. Deliberation, thought, and effort go into problem solving activities. Information obtained is evaluated in terms of accuracy, completeness, as well as being vital. This makes it possible to modify, refute, or accept the original hypothesis. Problem solving may be individual or within a committee setting. If collective work is stressed, ideas circulate within the committee members and are freely discussed with the intent of finding the best solution. Solutions to problems need to be shared within the classroom as well as with others. School newsletters sent home may include items of interest such as problem solving and project methods of study, among others in the total curriculum. Quality communication between home and school assists in working together for the good of the learner. Parents need to be invited to visit school and see social studies displays and activities. They might well reflect upon how to optimize achievement in knowledge, skills, and attitudes (See Cooper, 2009).

Electronic photos of student work in the social studies may displayed on bulletin board settings as well as outside the classroom hall. Pupil pride in accomplishments provide ample opportunities for metacognitive reflection. Metacognition then provides situations whereby evaluation of achievement occurs. Thus, the learner appraises how well something was attained as well as ways to improve learnings. Gaps in learning, too, are perceived with the end result being to acquire what is lacking. Curiosity in desiring to achieve results in doing extra credit work as in developing a book report or chart (narrative, classification, organizational, and/or agricultural products), related to a topic in an ongoing lesson/unit of study. Reading experiences should extend learnings whereby the learner relates content read to the self, to other texts and topics, and to others in society. Relationship of knowledge, ideas, and abilities makes for holism in learning (See Bonds-Raacke and Raacke, 2008).

Portfolios and Evaluation in the Social Studies

A major approach in assessing pupil progress might well be a portfolio procedure. Here, the pupil with teacher guidance collects products of his/her work and develops a portfolio of vital accomplishments. A representative sampling of dated entires is then placed into the portfolio. A table of contents gives order to the entries of a pupil which include

- diagrams, charts, illustrations, tables and graphs, as well as maps;
- summaries, reports, outlines, and letters;
- electronic photos of construction activities, art activities, projects, murals, models made, committees at work, and relief maps developed;
- recordings of oral communication experiences (See Vygotsky, 1978).

Contents in the portfolio provide ample opportunities for reflection and sharing with parents of the involved pupil. Here, the pupil as well as the teacher may describe progress in terms of the dated entries. Actual products are observed and not test scores only. Observers may evaluate what is done well as well as what needs improvement. Diagnosis and remediation are then inherent. Self evaluation by the pupil is stressed, with a reflective emphasis. Then too, the pupil is engaged in oral communication between a sender and a receiver. Active pupil engagement, interest, and purpose are salient factors in the evaluation process.

Additional assessment procedures to use are valid and reliable teacher written tests, learner participation in discussions, as well as observation of attitudes and feelings. However, the emphasis should be placed upon what the learner knows and does in everyday course work.

REFERENCES

Ahmad, Sajjad (2009), "Evolving a Framework for Teaching and Learning," *Edutracks*,, 8 (9), 11-12.

Bonds-Raacke, Jennifer, and John D. Raacke (2008), Using Table PCs in the Classroom: An Investigation of Student's Expectations and Reactions," *Journal of Instructional Psychology*, 35 (3), 235-239

Cooper, Patricia M. (2009), "Children's Literature for Reading Strategy-Instruction, Innovation, or Interference?, *Language Arts*, 86 (3), 178-187.

Ediger, Marlow (2009), "Supervising the Student Teacher in the Public School," *Education*, 130 (2), 251-254.

Ediger, Marlow (2009), "Seven Criteria for an Effective Classroom Environment," *College Student Journal*, 43 (4), 1370-1372.

Parsons, Seth (2008), "Providing all Students Access to Self Regulated Literacy Learning," *The Reading Teacher*, 61 (8), 628-636.

Vygotsky, L S. (1978), *Mind in Society: The Development of Higher Psychological Processes*. Cambridge, Massachusetts: Harvard University Press.

21

Portfolios in the Social Studies

There are a plethora of ways to show pupil achievement in the socil studies, one of which is the portfolio. Portfolio evaluation follows the thinking of constructivists who place major emphasis upon the pupil as an individual. Here, the pupil with teacher assistance is involved in selecting the entries. A table of contents provides structure for its contents. The portfolio is a flexible means of appraisal. Numerical results in terms of percentiles are not given in the assessment process. Instead, pupil progress may be viewed directly from authentic sources, such as products from the learner. A rubric may be utilized to appraise the portfolio and agreed upon standards used by evaluators to provide for interscorer reliability. The portfolio permits responsible observers to notice achievement as well as what is left to learn.

There are numerous kinds of products which may be placed into a social studies portfolio. Each entry reveals what has been emphasized in ongoing lessons and units of study.

Selecting Products for the Portfolio

The pupil with teacher guidance must carefully choose which representative products should become a part of the portfolio. These products represent the work of a specific pupil and should not only satisfy the child but also communicate achievement. They indicate progress of dated entries and might well show sequentially how well a pupil is doing in school. The learner owns the portfolio and should feel pride in its accomplishments. The following entries, among others, need to be included with an accompanying Table of Contents showing the work of the child:

- electronic illustrations of art work, murals, construction items, and other projects completed in the social studies;
- photos of committees, including the involved pupil, participating in problem solving experiences;
- graphs (line, bar, circle), tables containing data from diverse units of study, charts developed (organizational, pedigree, narrative, classification), drawings made, time lines, and diagrams;
- videos of dramatics participation (creative, informal, and formal) in social studies units of study;
- recordings of oral book reports, debates, reader's theatre and committee endeavours;
- written summaries, outlines, poems written, and reports.

Each of the above portfolio entries may contribute much to successful parent/teacher conferences. By viewing and evaluating learner products, parents may assess authentic achievements. Questions may well be raised and discussions follow. Agreements might be made on specifics parents can help in to foster pupil progress. Reflection is necessary to notice additional assistance needed with learners, also, being actively involved in the evaluation process. This should motivate pupil progress. An effective social studies curriculum must meet the needs of pupils individually and collectively.

Pupils differ from each other in myriad ways including abilities, interests, and attitudes. Thus, the teacher needs to consider a plethora of factors when assisting pupil learning in the social studies (Ediger, 2009).

Constructivism in the Social Studies

Constructivism, as a psychology of learning, emphasizes that pupils, individually, construct their very own knowledge and this is modified as ensuing lessons and units of study progress. Knowledge and skills then do not remain static, but are subject to change and modification. The teacher guides, motivates, and encourages learning, but does not dictate, lecture, or reprimand pupils to achieve. He/she facilitates learning. Self motivation by the pupil is salient and is assisted by others to grow, develop, and learn. Responsibility for learning rests upon the pupil. When the teacher notices pupils, in ongoing lessons and units of study, experience difficulties, he/she provides learnings to overcome problem areas. Thus, a teacher may not directly answer a pupil's question, but offer assistance on where to locate the needed information. Then too, the teacher might, in response to a pupil's question, raise related questions, leading the pupil to the necessary response. Inductive learning is heavily stressed whereby pupils learn by discovery. Learning is an active process. The teacher assists at the time a pupil faces a dilemma and this helps the learner to establish equilibrium, as well as move forward in achieving holism (See Wolk, 2008).

Constructivism is somewhat opposite of behaviourism which is commonly stressed in the curriculum. Behaviourism emphasizes that objectives of instruction be established prior to instruction. The objectives can be clarified by having the teacher state what is expected of learners as a result of teaching. They are specific and leave little/no leeway for interpretation. Pupils then generally know what is expected of them. This provides security to learners. After instruction has occurred, the teacher may test pupils to notice if successful teaching has occurred and pupils have achieved stated objectives. Measurement is very important to behaviourists.

For teacher written tests, the percent of correct answers is noticed. With state mandated testing, pupil's scores can be show with percentiles. For example, out of every one hundred pupils tested, 65 are below and 35 above for a learner who scored on the 65th percentile. Precision is involved with pupils either being correct/incorrect on multiple choice test items taken on a mandated test or for a teacher written test (See Rose, 1999).

Behaviourism emphasizes that learning opportunities be aligned with the stated objectives so that pupils have a better chance at success. The teacher may then directly teach so that pupils achieve objectives and are successful in achieving. E. L. Thorndike in the early 1900s emphasized selected basic philosophical principles of behaviourism:

- whatever exists, exists in some amount
- if it exists in some amount, it can be measured.

These beliefs brought the testing movement into vogue with tests being developed in a plethora of areas such as academic achievement in different curriculum areas, vocational skills, attitudes, personality development, among others. Measurement was a key concept here and in present day schools, testing is the rule rather than the exception. Tracking of pupil progress stresses the importance of viewing test scores over a period of time to notice progress over previous times of measurement, during the public school years. Is progress being made by the involved learner?

With computer use, mass numbers of pupil test results may be evaluated in a short period of time. These can be retrieved and shown readily on a monitor, for evaluation by teachers, principals, supervisors, superintendents of schools, as well as other responsible persons (See Eddy, 1997). There are questions to be raised pertaining to behaviourism as a psychology of learning:

- How appropriate is it to minimize pupil questions when emphasizing predetermined objectives of instruction? The objectives then are stated prior to instruction and with aligned learning activities determine what is taught.

- With highly precise objectives, does teaching stress pupils learn specific facts which can be measured through multiple choice test items? Responses to multiple choice test items require exact answers with no leeway for pupil thought.
- Do teachers teach toward pupils doing well on tests rather than higher levels of cognition?
- With pupils zooming in on the correct answer, does this approach minimize creative thinking possibilities?

Test results can be incorporated into a portfolio, along with those mentioned above for constructivist psychology of instruction (See Gardner, 1993).

REFERENCES

Eddy, John, *et.al.* (1997), Technology Assisted Instruction, *Education*,117 (3), 478-480.

Ediger, Marlow (2009), "Supervising the Student Teacher in the Public School," *Education*, 130 (2), 251-254.

Gardner, Howard (1993), *Multiple Intelligences: Theory and Practice.* New York: Basic Books.

Rose, M. (1999), *"Ten Easy Writing Lessons That Get Kids Ready for Writing Assessments,"* New York; Scholastic.

Wolk, S. (2008), "Joy in School," *Educational Leadership*, 66 (1), 8-14.

22 Mentoring in the Social Studies

Quality social studies instruction is salient for all pupils.What happens on the local, state, national, and international levels affect each person. Then too, social studies should emphasize good citizenship in school and in society. A knowledgeable person with needed skills to function well in relating to others is important. People possess different values, beliefs, and cultures which indicate that each person must be accepting of others and stress a caring society. The social studies mentor might well assist the teacher in improving the curriculum involving objectives, learning activities, and appraisal procedures in ongoing lessons and units of study.

Defining the Role of the Mentor

Mentors must be well-versed in teaching the social studies as well as apply appropriate psychological principles in ongoing lessons and units of study. They need to be able to work effectively with each teacher, using quality human relations. Being uncaring, rude, and arrogant have no roles to play in teaching and learning situations. Cooperatively, the mentor and teacher need to identify problematic situations and work harmoniously in their solution(s). There are situations which hinder learner progress in the social studies. These must be pinpointed and resolved to assist pupils to achieve more optimally:

(1) pupils not understanding vital concepts and generalizations. Here, the mentor and the teacher must analyze reasons for this occurring. A variety of developmentally appropriate experiences need to be in the offing. These must be sequenced so that more optimal achievement does occur. The pace of lesson presentations should be such that acquisition of concepts and generalizations are attained with meaning theory being emphasized. Continual diagnosis need to be stressed so that learner achievement is in evidence (See Wolk, 2008).

(2) pupils need assistance in scaffolding. When learnings appear to be too complex, within reason, the teacher perceives a gap between what the pupil is achieving and what might be possible To close the identified gap, a series of carefully ordered learnings may make for closure (Ediger, 2010).

(3) pupils need to be engaged in ongoing lessons and units of study. With involvement, pupils perceive interest in achieving salient objectives. The learner and the curriculum become one with the interest factor inherent in learning. There are fewer distractions and less lack of time on task, when each pupil is focussed on the learning activity at hand. Disruptions in learning need to be replaced with interesting experiences in the social studies (See Parsons, 2008).

(4) pupils must feel that purpose is involved in pursuing, growing, and developing. Meaningless subject matter consisting of facts and trivia must be replaced with vital concepts and generalizations. The mentor and the social studies teacher cooperatively need dialogue to come up with what is worthwhile and purposeful to the learner (See Young and Gates, 2005)

(5) pupil self monitoring stresses the importance of learner ownership of the curriculum. Thus, the pupil reflects upon what has been acquired and comes up with more accurate ideas in terms of subject matter learnings.

The mentor is a guide and motivator in assisting each teacher to put forth maximum effort in teaching and learning situations. He/she does not dictate nor force selected behaviours upon the teacher, but rather intrinsically helps social studies teachers to analyze teaching behaviours with the intent of providing pupils with challenging, developmentally appropriate experiences. The mentor must be highly knowledgeable about different philosophies of instruction in order to provide the best fit for individual styles of learning. Mandated objectives are predetermined and measurably stated, for teachers to use in teaching and learning situations. These ends represent targets to aim toward in the instructional arena. Learning activities are aligned with the precise objectives. After instruction, the teacher may measure to ascertain if the specific objective(s) have been achieved. Generally, it is an either/or situation if the objective has been attained by the learner. There is little/no leeway in the interpretation of any objective. In contrast, constructivism stresses that the pupil sequences his/her own experiences. Thus, for example, in an ongoing social studies lesson, pupil(s) with teacher guidance identify a problem area. The problem is delimited so it can be solved. An hypothesis, or tentative answer, is developed. Learners then seek reference materials for possible solutions. A variety of relevant sources need to be used such as AV materials, knowledgeable resource personnel, internet and world wide web data, as well as traditional reading sources including reputable basal textbooks and library books. This provides ample opportunities to evaluate subject matter from the different sources of information to come up with an answer to the identified problem area. The hypothesis is then accepted, modified, or refuted. In the problem solving arena, the learner then sequences his/her own experiences. There are no specifically arranged objectives for pupil attainment along the spectrum. Instead, constructivism, represented here by problem solving, is holistic whereby there is a general framework, which is very open ended, leaving room for pupil initiative, creativity, and critical thought. At each ordered step along the way, the pupil with teacher assistance aids the pupil in the involved process toward completion. The pupil is responsible for quality work in problem solving and owns the curriculum together with the teacher. There is no lecture and no predetermined objectives; flexibility is involved in the learner following through on broad guidelines in problem solving. The mentor then must be highly educated in different philosophies of instruction including the use of measurable stated objectives *versus* constructivism with in-between points being possible (Ediger, 2010).

Many experts in social studies instruction praise the merits of small group learning as compared to individual endeavours. Here, learning style choices and preferences vary among pupils. The mentor and the social studies teacher need to evaluate which works best for learners. Perhaps, there must be rational balance between the two procedures due to individuals needing to work collectively as well as individually in school and in society. With either approach, the teacher needs to observe that all are on task and achieving (See Kielsmeier, 2010).

With the collective or individual endeavour, the teacher and mentor might desire to have pupils complete a written/oral report on a nation of their own choosing in a unit, for example, on the Middle East. A committee of learners or a pupil individually may choose the nation of Jordan. This nation, among others, in the Middle East might have received short shrift in the basal textbook. With utilization of the internet, resource personnel, printed items and articles, as well as audio-visual materials, pupils may glean the following pertaining to Jordan:

- the capitol city of Amman contains a Roman Amphitheatre in mint condition, seating approximately 6,000 people.

- the importance of Petra, located 140 miles south of Amman, is situated in a ravine with either sides containing beautiful carvings in the rose red rock limestone. Selected carvings include Pharoah's Treasury House, a monastery, buildings that were used to sell produce from rural areas, as well as laid out streets. Petra was at its zenith 100 BC to 100 AD. Nearby are active springs which provide an ample supply of water. Petra is truly a tourist mecca.
- two castles, Kerak and Shobeck in their original condition, were built in the days of the Crusades, in which numerous Crusaders settled along the way in going to the Holy Land. Both castles, located between Amman and Petra, contain a Nobleman's quarters and a large dining hall. Servants and horses were also kept in these castles.
- Jerash, located forty miles north of Amman, has beautifully lined streets of tall columns on either side leading to the remains of a large building dedicated to their God, Artemis. The writer has visited Jerash numerous times and has a well done painting of this ancient city hanging on the wall. Jerash was built in a desert and water flowed by gravity for a distance of thirty miles to meet human needs in the days of the Roman Empire. A breaking of the canal could bring ruins to Jerash and turn it into a desert.
- the modern University of Jordan, is located in Amman. It has a medical school from which its graduates practice medicine in different regions of the world. The University trains professionals in different areas of specialization.
- a plethora of bedouin tribes live in semi-desert areas of Jordan. They keep their possessions light so movement is readily possible to areas suitable for grazing by camels, sheep, and goats. The bedouin are very hospitable and the writer has eaten numerous meals in their tents. Meat is scarce and served during

important events such as Ramadan, the holiest month of the Islamic calendar in which the devout go to Mecca, Saudi Arabia once in a lifetime unless handicaps and hardships hinder. When eating in a bedouin tent with no tables nor chairs, the writer sat on the ground in a circle with a platter of rice and lamb's meat in the middle of approximately eight persons. The hands are used in eating with no knives, forks, and spoons available. Hot tea was served as a beverage. Water is scarce and is largely used to wash hands, face, and feet in performing ablutions, prior to prayer said five times a day, always facing Mecca.

- a sixth century mosaic map in Medeba, thirty miles south of Amman, is located in the Church of St. George. This map of Jerusalem and its surroundings was developed when the Byzantines ruled the Holy Land region. They had their beginning with Constantine the Great (330 AD) and stressed the Greek Orthodox Christian beliefs (Ediger, 1999).

The nation of Jordan has survived a myriad of difficulties. Jordan is composed of sixty per cent Palestinian Arabs who came in as refugees from the West Bank of the Jordan River when Israel became a state in 1948 on eighty per cent of the land formerly known as Palestine. The writer served as a teacher and relief worker with the Mennonite Central Committee,1952-1954, and he assisted in clothing distribution to Palestinian refugees after the 1948 war in Aqaba Camp, directly south of Jericho. Clay huts, unemployed people, and no sanitary system existed in this camp; these refugees fled to the nation of Jordan during and after the 1967 six day war in which Israel captured the rest of the land of Palestine. Some of these have integrated into Jordanian society while others live in refugee camps. Jordan took in another one million Iraqi refugees during the US invasion of Iraq during the 2000-2010 decade. Where does Jordan secure the resources to meet needs of refugees? The United Nation Relief and Works Agency provided very minimum aid for each refugee. There are well known personalities gleaned from Jordanian history such as King Abdulla, the first king of Jordan, 1948-1951. His grandson King Hussein governed from 1952 until his death in 1999. King Hussein's son King Abdulla the 2nd has ruled since that time. These kings claim direct descent from the Prophet Mohammed (570-632).

Key ideas have been providing for teaching about Jordan. Mentors should assist teachers to emphasize structural ideas in teaching. A variety of learning experiences need provision to meet needs of individual pupils. Mentors who majored in the social sciences have myriad opportunities to assist teachers in choosing key ideas for teaching and learning situations. They also must have a plethora of suggested procedures as learning activities and evaluation procedures (See Medina and Costa, 2010).

REFERENCES

Ediger, Marlow and D. Bhaskara Rao (2010), *Effective School Curriculum*. New Delhi, India: Discovery Publishing House.

Ediger, Marlow (2010), "Constructivism and the Social Studies," *Edutracks*, 9 (7), 13-14. Published in India.

Ediger, Marlow (1999), *The Holy Land*. Kirksville, Missouri: Simpson Publishing Company.

Kielsmeier, James C. (2010), "Build a Bridge Between Service and Learning," *Phi Delta Kappan*, 91 (5), 8-15).

Medina, Carmen, and Maria Del Rocio Costa, "Collaborative Voices Exploring Culturally and Socially Responsive Literacies," *Language Arts*, 87 (4), 263-276.

Parsons, Seth A. (2008), "Providing All Students with Access to Self Regulated Learning," The Reading Teacher, 61 (98), 628-635.

Wolk, S. (2008), "Joy in School," *Educational Leadership*, 66 (1), 8-14.

Young, Raymond, and Carl M. Cates (2005), "Playful Communication in Mentoring," *College Student Journal*, 39 (4), 692-701.

Revisiting the Scope and Sequence in the Social Studies

With federal mandates in education (No Child Left Behind), social studies instruction was greatly minimized since it was not tested in pupil achievement. Restoring social studies to its rightful place is salient due to its relevance for pupils. Quality citizenship should be a major objective of instruction and this concept may be integrated in all of its study. Being a good citizen in school and in society is necessary for optimal achievement to occur. Disruptive behaviour, rudeness, and impoliteness have no roles to play in a quality curriculum.

The social studies teacher has an important responsibility to determine with other teachers the breadth and depth (scope) as well as order (sequence) of units to be taught on a given grade level. Planning each lesson and unit of study is salient so that pupils achieve more optimally in the school setting (Ediger, 2007).

Planning the Framework in the Social Studies

Scope will be discussed first. What will be decided upon as the breadth of subject matter to be emphasized in ongoing lessons and units of study? If, for example, a unit on the

Middle East is being considered, which concepts and generalizations will be stressed as objectives of instruction? The social studies teacher may choose to include the nations of Jordan, Israel, and the West Bank, as part of a unit of study on the Middle East. The following might be key structural ideas identified in terms of knowledge objectives:

- the West Bank of the Jordan River was a part of the nation of Jordan from 1948 until 1967;
- the West Bank contains 20 per cent of the land formerly called Palestine. Thus 80 per cent became the nation of Israel in 1948. A ceasefire in this Arab/Israeli war set the boundaries in 1948;
- in 1967, Israel captured the rest of the West Bank from Jordan in what is known as the six day war;
- the walled city of Jerusalem was located on the West Bank. This wall, the third in its history, was completed in 1542 when the Ottoman Empire governed the land of Palestine from 1517-1917. The Ottoman Empire was defeated in World War One. Great Britain received the League of Nations Mandate to rule the land of Palestine in 1922, after the negotiations were completed following World War One;
- The walled city contains salient sites important to Islam, Judaism, and Christianity. The Dome of the Rock, an octagonal building with a gold plaited dome, was built in 691 AD, after the Muslims captured the land of Palestine. It houses Mount Moriah, the site where the Patriarch Abraham was tempted to offer as a sacrifice his son Isaac, according to Judaism, whereby, in Islam, Abraham was tempted to sacrifice his son Ishmael. Isaac is considered the father of Judaism, and Ishmael, the father of the Arab nations. From the Dome, a Muezzin calls devout Muslims to prayer five times a day; also nearby, the Prophet Mohammed made his midnight journey into heaven and came back to earth again, according to devout followers of Islam;

- the Western Wall, located adjacent to the Dome of the Rock, is the only remains of the ancient Jewish temple, built during the days of Herod the Great. Here, devout Jews come to pray daily. Herod the Great ruled Palestine from 30 BC to 3 BC. when the Roman Empire was at its zenith in power;
- inside the walled city is the Church of the Holy Sepulcher which houses the Tomb of Christ. The Church was built by the Crusaders in 1142 after they had captured most of the Holy Land from the Muslims in 1099. It houses also the place of one of three crosses from which Christ was crucified, according to devout beliefs of Christians (Ediger, 1998).

The walled city of Jerusalem was a part of the nation of Jordan until Israel captured it along with the West Bank in the 1967 six day war. The above asterisked items may be stated as objectives for pupil attainment. The scope might well be broadened to include the Sea of Galilee, as well as the Dead Sea, among many, many others. For example, in the northwest where the Dead Sea and the Jordan river intersect are the remains of the Esscenes, a communal, religious group who separated themselves from others. The remains show a communal kitchen where Esscene members shared meals, a scriptorium room for writing religious texts, a storage area for food, and sleeping quarters. Stone slabs were slept upon with stone pillows to elevate the head. Even with scant rainfall of less than five inches a year, the Esscenes each day followed a purification ritual by dipping into an adjacent pool. Esscene society came to an end, approximately 100 AD, when the Roman Army captured this settlement.

The scope of the social studies must be carefully determined. The breadth of subject matter to be emphasized in teaching and learning situations adequately delimits a unit of study to be stressed in ongoing lessons and units of study. This makes for a planned balance in content from the social sciences with other social studies units (See Parker, 2001).

Sequence in the Social Studies

Equally poignant is the concept of sequence. Here, the teacher determines the order of units to be taught as well as sequential learning activities to be emphasized within a unit of study. The writer, here, will discuss the order of learning activities to be provided within a unit. Thus, the teacher must provide for individual differences among learners so that each might attain optimally. Scaffolding is salient in that a pupil or group might well attain a higher level than what is developmentally appropriate. For example, the pupil may be able to achieve objective A, but objective B is too complicated unless scaffolding is used as a teaching strategy. With scaffolding, the teacher assists pupils to attain more optimally with a series of learning opportunities which challenge the pupil to realize higher levels of achievement in smaller steps. The social studies teacher must carefully evaluate pupil achievement within a lesson to help when this becomes necessary. Teacher observation is very important when teaching pupils to notice where assistance is necessary. Inductively, the teacher may raise questions which lead a pupil to a more accurate understanding of subject matter or a skill when the learner needs guidance (National Council for the Social Studies, 1997).

The social studies teacher has selected guidelines to follow in teaching to optimize sequential pupil progress:

- pupils need to be actively involved in learning. Distractions hinder achievement and progress. The classroom climate must be such that it encourages learning. Rules need to be established and communicated clearly to learners. Violations need to be treated in a humane way. The social studies teacher must think of methods of discipline which encourage learning and achievement. Active involvement in learning means that the interests of pupils must be considered. There are methods to make any topic or lesson interesting. Vary the kinds of experiences provided and include stimulating discussions, use of age appropriate audio-visual materials, art work to indicate what has been acquired in knowledge objectives, dramatizations to assist in history becoming alive, divide pupils up into doing committee work for peer mediated critical and creative thinking activities, among others. Observe off task behaviours to secure learner participation. Use of voice inflection guides pupils to be increasingly attentive. Active participation in learning improves sequence within the pupil (see Guilfoyle, Christy (2006).

- pupils must become motivated to attain ordered objectives within lessons and units of study. Increased energy levels are then available for pupils to devote to tasks being pursued. Social studies teachers must study each pupil's behaviour to notice that which motivates such as project methods, problem solving experiences, reading/reporting on library books read, choice of activities at a learning centre in the classroom, small group work, among others. Intrinsic motivation generally works best; however some pupils feel motivation through extrinsic means.With intrinsic motivation, pupils perceive purpose in learning. Reasons are sensed for participating in an ongoing activity or within a unit of study. The motivation then comes from within the pupil. Extrinsic motivation stresses the importance of external rewards being necessary to feel the need for learning. They may consist of inexpensive awards such as an inked, rubber stamp of a turkey during the month of November for each correct item, for example, in a workbook exercise. The ratio may be increased to one stamped response for every five correct items. Extrinsic motivation aids selected learners to achieve sequentially in a more optimal manner (See Parsons, 2008).
- pupils need to learn what is relevant. With relevancy, learners feel that what is acquired is practical and updated. A quality current events programme makes for discussing vital, every day happenings. Newscasts

from radio and TV, news magazines and newspapers, along with the internet provide relevant items for discussion. The writer uses a search engine to type in the following entries to secure news from nations of the Middle East: the Jordan Times, The Damascus (Syria) News, the Tehren (Iran) Times, and the Jerusalem Post. Pupils might then read and discuss sequential happens from Middle Eastern Nations. Reading news happenings form other nations is exciting and fascinating. The social studies teacher must be certain that pupils possess background information to benefit from the new learnings (Ediger, 2002).

- pupil self selection of library books, directly related to the ongoing unit of study assists learners to sequence their very own experiences. They tend to choose books which are of interest and on their reading level. The library books need to be informational, but there are selected quality narrative reading materials which pique interests and are fictional, but also related to the unit being stressed. The writer has known several individuals with high interest and knowledge in history which was acquired through reading historical novels. When these books are read during class time in Sustained Silent Reading (SSR), pupils improve in word recognition skills and subject matter knowledge. Words not recognized while reading may be ascertained by using context clues our phonics. Learners may do most sequencing in reading library books on their very own. Ideas read may be brought into small group or classroom discussions as they relate to the concepts and generalizations being emphasized. When supervising university student teachers in the public schools, the writer has noticed in selected observations that pupils' ideas from library book reading were used as a basis for discussion rather than the basal textbook. Pupil enthusiasm and contributions indicated that this was an enjoyable experience. Here, pupils need to respect the ideas of others (See Ross, 2008).

There are selected concepts which are salient to stress when sequence in learning is operationalized:

- *advance organizers*. They assist pupils to understand what is taught whereby the social studies teacher presents subject matter which assists pupils to attach meaning to that which follows in the lesson/unit of study. A stimulating and brief prerequisite experience then is follow by the implemented lesson plan.
- *metacognition*. This concept refers to thinking about thinking. Thus, pupils are aided to recall and think about what was taught, leading to higher levels of cognition including critical and creative thinking. These processes help pupils to order ideas in promoting sequential learnings.
- *self efficacy*. With sequential learnings, pupils develop a repertoire of salient subject matter in ongoing social studies lessons and units of study. Confidence is then achieved in attaining vital concepts and generalizations. Building blocks from previous social studies encounters assist in achieving new objectives. Feelings of adequacy might well come about due to relating the new with previously acquired subject matter and skills.
- *success in learning*. Pupils tend to like the social studies when they feel positively toward teaching and learning situations. Success in achievement is poignant. With success, the motivation is there to increase opportunities for social studies learnings. The self concept should thrive. Feelings of failure accrue when the self concept becomes minimized. Learnings which are too complex make for negative feelings and frustration, whereas content which is too easy might make for feelings of boredom (See Vygotsky, 1978).

REFERENCES

Dunn, Boss E. (2008), 'The Two World Histories," *Social Education*, 72 (5), 257-263.

Ediger Marlow and D. Bhaskara Rao (2007), *Teaching the Social Studies.* New Delhi, India: Discovery Publishing House.

Ediger, Marlow (1998), *The Holy Land.* Kirksville, Missouri: Simpson Publishing Company.

Ediger, Marlow (2002), Current Events in the Social Studies," *Edutracks*, 7(3), 14-15.

Guifoyle, Christy (2006), NCLB: Is There Life Beyond Testing?" *Educational Leadership*, 64 (3), 8-13.

National Council for the Social Studies (1997), Curriculum Standards for the Social Studies. Edison, New York: Whitehurst and Clark.

Parker, Walter C. (2001), *Social Studies in Elementary Education.* Upper Saddle River, New Jersey: Merrill, Prentice Hall.

Parsons, Seth A. (2008), "Providing All Students Aces to Self Regulated Learning," *The Reading Teacher*, 61 (1), 8-14.

Vygotsky, L. S. (1978), Mind in Society: The Development of Higher Psychological Processes. Cambridge, Massachusetts: Harvard University Press.

24

Children's Literature in the Social Studies Curriculum

There are myriad library books written for children which may be incorporated into ongoing lessons and units in the social studies. These are written on different topics that individually may relate directly to objectives of instruction in the classroom setting. Library books need to be on diverse reading levels in order for a pupils to select one which is developmentally appropriate. The social studies teacher must briefly tell about salient books that might well pique learner attention. Then too, the teacher may read aloud to children, during story time, a carefully chosen book which captures pupils' interests. Thus, there is much social studies subject matter that pupils may acquire from library book content (See Ellery, 2010).

Library Book Content in the Social Studies

A neat, well developed colourful bulletin board draws pupil attention to salient library books. While supervising university student teachers in the public schools, the writer observed four committee members plan and complete a library book bulletin board display. Crepe paper of red and green provided the outline. The caption was titled, "Enjoying the Social Studies and Library Books." Jackets of new books were posted on the bulletin board. Underneath each was a brief description of the library book. The teacher introduced each book briefly as she pointed to the related book jacket. Proper voice inflection can do much to capture pupil interest. Thus, appropriate stress, pitch, and enunciation, entices learner attention. Not only new books may be introduced, but also fascinating older library copies should receive attention in the classroom. There are favourites among pupils which are read by a plethora of young learners. Bulletin boards should be changed frequently to encourage pupil reading. They may be developed by the teacher at the beginning of a school year. When readiness occurs, pupil/teacher planning might be used as well as a committee of learners being engaged in planning and doing these bulletin boards. Being on the lookout for bulletin board ideas is poignant to social studies teachers (See Wyss, 2007).

There are numerous plans for having children read library books as well as methods of achievement evaluation:

- pupils choose and read library books from selections made by the teacher or school librarian, devoted to the social studies. The teacher observes which books and by whom these are read. Teacher observation and related records kept might be a good way to assess progress. There are pupils who thrive in an informal programme of reading library books in the social studies.
- pupils select and read a library book and then have a brief conference with the social studies teacher. A random sampling of conferences provide much feedback on reading comprehension from questions asked by the teachers as well as word recognition skills shown by a pupil in oral reading. The teacher dates and records specific information. Streamlining the approach makes for efficiency in the conference setting.
- pupils share ideas gleaned from reading library books during time devoted to the social studies, especially if

they relate to an ongoing lesson/unit of study (Ediger, 2010).

There are selected procedures available in assisting pupils who have difficulties in word recognition. Procedures must be adapted to the developmental level of the learner and include the following:

- *use of context clues*. Thus, an unknown word needs to harmonize in meaning with the rest of the words in the sentence or paragraph. Sometimes, a pupil will place a word in context which is ridiculous and does not make sense. Pupils may be aided in inserting a word which is meaningful for the unknown.
- *use of phonics*. Initial consonants, in particular, identified properly, provide strong clues in word recognition especially if used with context clues. They are generally very consistent in relating symbol and sound.
- use of picture clues which are heaviest in literature for young children. If a pupil is not able to recognize a word, the picture on the same page of print will fill in for the unknown.
- use of teacher or proficient pupil reader in pronouncing words for those who have difficulties in word recognition. Pupils should not lose interest in reading due to not identifying unknown words. Assisting pupils, almost immediately, in identifying the unknown, helps in reading comprehension (Ediger, 2007).

Comprehension of Subject Matter

There are pupils who read words but do not understand the inherent ideas. They are word callers and do not comprehend what has been read. It is good for the social studies teacher to periodically ask a pupil to say in his/her own words what was understood from his/her reading. Recalling, literally, subject matter read is a beginning point in comprehension. This needs to be stressed prior to emphasizing higher levels of comprehension. Recall of subject matter, ideally, must be operationalized when actual reading of words is being in evidence. Reading is worthless unless ideas are being gleaned. Cause and effect is next in complexity in comprehension and is enclosed in historical content. Thus for example in a unit on the Middle East, there are causes for effects such as the Palestinian/Israeli disagreements over the land of Palestine. Critical thinking, in sequence, must also be stressed. For example, how have previous plans failed in coming up with a solution to highly relevant situations? This is making comparisons in procedures and approaches. Creative thinking, also salient, would differ in that the pupil needs to come up with a unique solution between opposing sides in the conflict. There are additional types of thinking including

- reading between the lines where the subject matter is not clear cut, as in reading population figures in growth between Arab *versus* Israelis which show population data by decades. What do these trends indicate? How will these data influence future developments between opposing sides?
- reading to make comparisons and contrasts such as what are the differences between Judaism and Islam in religious beliefs. For instance, once in a person's lifetime, Islam requires devout followers, unless illness or handicap prevent, to make a tour during the Holy month of Ramadan to Mecca, in Saudi Arabia. Mecca is their holiest city and the birth place of Mohammed (570-631 AD.) The title of Hajj is given to participants. In contrast, devout followers of Judaism face Jerusalem, their holiest city, when praying. The Western Wall is the only remnant of the ancient Jewish temple in Jerusalem and is a salient site for prayers (Ediger, 1999).
- reading to make predictions. This may be a complex type of reading, especially when predicting the future of a Palestinian nation since many Jewish settlements have been built on the West Bank which Israel captured from the nation of Jordan in the 1967 six day war. The thinking needed here, emphasizes complex considerations (Seek internet information on the World Wide Web for content on the Palestinians and Israel).

Reading subject matter from basal social studies textbooks involves several readiness factors. The new vocabulary terms need to be introduced and observed on the white board. The act of reading becomes more meaningful when pupils view these concepts and discuss their meaning. All pupils should see the words clearly in order to recognize them while reading silently or aloud from the basal textbook. During the discussion, pupils raise questions which might be answered from reading the textbook selection. The salient questions, along with those of the teacher and printed on the white board, provide a structure for reading comprehension of subject matter. The possible questions, for example, might include the following:

- what is the name of the holy book of devout Muslims? The answer being the Koran, and is at the recall level of cognition.
- what is meant by the term 'ablutions' as performed by Muslims? These rites are done prior to praying while facing Mecca, and is at the comprehension level of cognition.
- how does Muslim beliefs emphasize assisting others in society? One of the Five Pillars of Islam stresses the giving of tithes which is given to the less fortunate in society. This stresses the level of application in the cognitive domain.
- why did the Crusaders (Christians) and Muslims battle for the West Bank and the walled city of Jerusalem, in particular, 1099 AD? This emphasizes the level of analysis in the cognitive domain. The motives of the Crusaders included securing the Church of the Holy Sepulchre where the crucifixion and resurrection of Christ took place, according to devout Christians. Devout Muslims wanted to keep the Dome of the Rock, an octagonal, dome shaped structure housing Mount Moriah, the place where the Patriarch Abraham was tempted to sacrifice his Ishmael. From the Dome of the Rock area, Mohammed made a midnight journey into heaven and returned to

earth again. In the level of analysis, pupils with teacher guidance may use a variety of reference sources to locate relevant information on the many motives of Crusaders *versus* Muslims wanting the Holy Land region.

- how might Islamic and Crusader beliefs be summarized? The cognitive level of synthesis is in evidence here whereby pupils tie together what has been acquired (See National Council for the Social Studies," 1997).

Conclusion

Children's literature in the social studies should be an integral part of unit planning and implementation in the curriculum. Relevant information needs to be sought which captures and holds learner attention. Learning opportunities need to make sense and be meaningful. Pupil purposes, also, need adequate consideration in curriculum development (See Parker, 2001).

REFERENCES

Ediger, Marlow (2010), "Constructivism and the Social Studies," *Edutracks*, 9(7), 13-14.

Ediger, Marlow (2007), "Meaning in Reading Instruction," *Reading Improvement*, 44 (4), 217-220.

Ediger, Marlow (1999), *The Holy Land.* Kirksville, Missouri: Simpson Publishing Company.

Ellery, Valerie (2010), "How Do We Teach Reading as a Strategic Decision Making Process?" *The Reading Teacher*, 63 (5), 434-436.

National Council for the Social Studies (1997), *Curriculum Standards for the Social Studies.* Edison, New York: Whitehurst and Clark.

Parker, Walter C., (2001), *Social Studies in Elementary Education.* Upper Saddle River, New Jersey: Merrill, Prentice Hall.

Wyss, Paul Alan (2007), "Solving the Problem of Distance Library Services," *College Student Journal*, 41 (4), 747-754.

Student Notebooks and the Social Studies

Students need to do well in keeping notebooks with entries on the present unit of study being emphasized. These entries assist pupils to summarize what has been learned as well as review previous subject matter studied. They, also, help students to review main ideas and subordinate ideas gleaned from the ongoing lessons and unit. Writing skills in notebook development need adequate emphasis and these promote learner achievement, useful in school and in society. Different major objectives are then attained in the curriculum pertaining to the cognitive domain as well as skills in written work (Ediger, 2010).

Social Studies Notebooks and the Learner

Social studies notebooks may be stressed in electronic form or in traditional procedures. The content therein must be chosen carefully by the involved student. Only salient items should be recorded and dated. One daily entry should include major generalizations. Thus in a unit on the Middle East, the student might record that the Holy Land is very mountainous with one area being level and suitable for cultivation. This area is the Plains of Esdraelen, a triangle being thirty miles, by thirty miles, by forty miles for each side in dimension. It is located directly southeast of the modern city of Haifa. Depending upon the developmental level of the student, the written work may continue with cultivated crops raised here, such as wheat and barley (Ediger and Rao.2010).

In the notebook, poetry related to the unit being studied may be recorded, such as the following unrhymed four line quatrain written by a talented sixth grader:

A Dairy Farm on the Kibbutz

Many Holstein cows wait to be milked and fed
With pipeline milking machines, the milk flows on
To the bulk holding tank waiting in the storage room
Where a truck will haul it away to a processing plant.

Many poems rhyme and pupils do enjoy writing this type of verse, written by a fifth grade pupil:

Tilling the Land on a Kibbutz

Tractors roar in disking and seeding the field
In hopes of growing crops with a high yield
The wheat and barley grew well and produce much
With feelings there was a magical touch.

In the above quatrain, lines one and two rhyme whereas lines three and four rhyme. Essential social studies content must be in each poem whether it be free verse, a couplet, triplet, quatrain, limerick, haiku, and/or tanka (See Tiedt, 1982, on poetry writing).

The notebook belongs to the involved learner with the teacher serving as a guide and stimulates achievement. The writer when supervising university student teachers in the public schools observed poetry writing as was emphasized in ongoing units of study, and as prerequisites, students must have experienced

- listening to and reading the type of poetry to be stressed in social studies units of study

- analyzing what makes for each type of poem to be written such as a limerick or a haiku
- being ready for writing poetry. Learnings always should be developmentally appropriate
- scaffolding used to achieve challenging objectives (See Risko and Dalhouse, 2010)

New vocabulary terms should be written in the notebook. Thus, students may experience the following pertaining to the Crusades in the Middle Ages:

- noblemen, serfs, hermits, and slaves
- the Church of the Holy Sepulcher, Mount Moriah, Synagogues, Muslims, monasteries, among other relevant terms
- castles, moats, peasants and armies

Each vocabulary item must be meaningful to the learner and make sense. Small illustrations (drawn; digital; and/or others) may be placed next to each entry in the social studies notebook. It also is good to have each vocabulary term be printed and placed on a classroom word wall. Many pupils will look at these words periodically and, thus, review and ask related questions. The notebook entries and the word wall are very important in assisting pupils in vocabulary development and retention of learnings (See NSTA Reports, May, 2010).

Assignments should also be included in a social studies notebook. Students should make it appoint to fulfill these requirements when due. Proper study habits must be encouraged a young age with sequential progress made in time. Note taking needs to be demonstrated by the teacher. A taped recording of discussion may provide the setting here. Students need to view the model carefully and be guided in note taking. Note taking skills are very poignant since students then might review and rehearse the content prior to each lesson. New subject matter presented provides background information for ensuing main and subordinate subject matter content. Notes also provide a salient basis in studying for an upcoming test. Summarizing information when taking notes is a relevant skill for attending university classes at a later time. The notes indicate what is perceived as being vital ideas from classroom presentations (See Medina and Costa, 2010).

The social studies note book may also contain information in graphic form. Bar graphs, for example, showing population growth of nations studied provide content on trends and assist students to infer what might be likely to accrue in time. Line graphs might reveal growth in goods and services produced yearly or during longer units of time by a specific nation or several countries studied in ongoing lessons and units of studies. Picture graphs may indicate the number of students attending school in a nation. When readiness is in evidence, circle graphs may be used to show relevant data on a certain topic (See Parker, 2001).

Charts made might well be incorporated into a notebook. Thus, the following charts, directly related to an ongoing unit of study may become a part of the notebook:

- a narrative chart with related illustrations and a brief description for each may contain sequential information on agricultural methods, *i.e.* disking the farm land, seeding the crop to be grown, harvesting the grain, and storing the harvested crops;
- a flow chart with related pictures showing change at a specific point, such as petroleum being refined and at different temperature readings providing kerosene, gasoline of different grades, diesel fuel, and home heating fuel;
- a foods chart showing traditional meals and delicacies eaten in the Middle East, *i.e.* Kousa (rice and lamb's meat cooked in an inside removed tomato, egg plant, among others), masche (rice cooked inside of grape leaves), as well as baklava, a well known desert. Dates and figs are also eaten;
- a classification chart with categories and related illustrations pertaining to well known structures inside

the walled city of Jerusalem such as (the Dome of the Rock, an octagonal mosque with a gold plated dome, built in 691 AD, covering Mount Moriah where the Patriarch Abraham was tempted to offer his son Ishmael according to devout Muslims); the Western Wall, holy to devout believers in Judaism, which is the only remnant of the ancient Jewish temple; the Church of the Holy Sepulcher, which contains the tomb of Christ, according to devout Christians. The classification chart might also include languages spoken, well known personalities, and digital pictures of art (See National Council for the Social Studies, 1997).

Children's literature containing informational books correlates well with ongoing units of study. A wide variety of selections need to be available on diverse reading levels to provide for individual differences. Different topics must, also, be there. For example, if a unit on the Middle East is being taught, then developmentally appropriate books need to be in the offing on topics such as urban living, the bedouin, village life, agriculture, manufacturing, desert life, and education. The social studies teacher needs to introduce selected library books enthusiastically with voice inflection. Also, social studies library books may be read aloud during story time. The teacher must evaluate if approaches used motivate pupils to read and achieve. Students may keep written reports of library books read. The reports need to be dated and a related bar graph kept to encourage more reading in time. The social studies teacher might well model writing a book report containing essential ideas gleaned. Students should pay careful attention to the model as it is presented sequentially. Students will be at diverse levels of accomplishments in reading library books and in writing reviews/summaries. High expectations, within reason, must be emphasized.

Digital illustrations of completed committee work might be included in the notebook. Also, a video tape would indicate the quality of oral interactions. Thus, the committee endeavours may reveal the following:

- how well each student stayed on the topic at hand
- contributions made by each member
- knowledge and skill presented which directly relate to the topic discussed
- respect and acceptance of others on the committee
- assisting the small group to move forward in the discussion setting.

The writer has presented selected ideas for learnings to become a part of a student's notebook. There are, of course, additional entries which may be included. The student's notebook should reveal what has been accomplished during a specific interval of time.

REFERENCES

Costa, Carmen I., and Maria del Rocio Costa, (2001), "Collaborative Voices Exploring Culturally and Socially Responsive Literacies," *Language Arts*, 87 (4), 263-276

Ediger, Marlow (2010), "Constructivism in the Social Studies," *Edutracks*, 9(7),13-14.

Ediger, Marlow, and D. Bhaskara Rao (2010), *The Effective School Curriculum*. New Delhi, India: Discovery Publishing House.

National Council for the Social Studies (1997), *Curriculum Standards for the Social Studies*. Edison, New York: Whitehurst and Clark.

NSTA Reports (May, 2010), "Enhancing Learning with Science Notebooks," Arlington, Virginia: National Science Teachers Association.

Parker, Walter C. (2001), *Social Studies in Elementary Education*. Upper Saddle River, New Jersey: Merrill, Prentice Hall.

Risko, Victoria, and Doris Walker-Dalhouse (2010), Reading Research into the Classroom," *The Reading Teacher*, 63 (5), 420-423.

Tiedt, Iris M. (1982), *The Language Arts Handbook*. Englewood Cliffs, New Jersey: Prentice Hall, Inc.

Oral Communication in the Social Studies

Oral communication skills are salient in all curriculum areas as well as in the societal realm. Social studies, as one academic discipline, can make definite contributions in assisting learners to effectively communicate with others. Of all language arts skills, orally communicating with others is the most frequently used in society. There need to be definite objectives in each unit of study as well as emphasis therein in daily lesson plans. How might oral communication be stressed in the social studies?

Learning Opportunities in the Social Studies

To provide for individual differences among pupils, variety is a key word here. Also, pupils are on different achievement levels, and this is a prime consideration in choosing objectives of instruction. Scaffolding must be included as a definitive possibility in oral communication when thinking of stressing high expectations in teaching and learning situations.

Discussions in ongoing units and lessons are important to include frequently. Within discussions, pupils are able to clarify ideas presented and attach related meanings. Higher levels of cognition such as critical and creative thinking need inclusion. At the same time quality in effective oral communication might well be emphasized. Proper stress, pitch, rate, and enunciation must be practiced by learners. The social studies teacher presents a role model here in each lesson taught where ideas circulate among members of the class and of the teacher to effectively present subject matter (Ediger, 2010).

Listening is an inherent part of quality communication. The listener needs to perceive purpose and pay careful attention to what is said. Periodic assessment of careful listening should become an integral part of the curriculum. Distractions must be eliminated and factors which facilitate communicator/listener should be enhanced. Respect for each pupil and his/her contributions need reinforcement. Rudeness and impolite behaviour must be eliminated with rational rules and regulations which are enforced. These standards of conduct may be planned with class members and under teacher supervision. Evaluation of pupil achievement in meeting these standards provides additional opportunities for purposeful oral communication (National Council for the Social Studies, 1997).

Small group collaboration is a method of teaching which provides individuals opportunities to participate more frequently. Here, pupils may practice staying on the social studies topic at hand. Active participation by all is needed to have the group move forward. Leadership may emerge as individuals ask for clarification of ideas and offer suggestions. Learners may scaffold content as challenges in thinking occur. Subject matter achievement accrues with high expectations from pupils, as well as the teacher, might well come about as a result of active pupil involvement. The topic my relate to the ongoing social studies unit and chosen by learners with teacher guidance. Practicing courtesy within a small group might well make for feelings of cohesion as well as respect for each other (See Guilfoyle, 2006).

A project method stresses the importance of developing construction and human relations skills. The project needs to be relevant to the involved learners. Careful planning of the construction experience is a must. The teacher needs to demonstrate orally how a project is chosen and planned. The carrying out of the plans emphasizes responsible behavior by those working on the project. Tools, materials, and equipment must be used and returned to their proper places before, during, and after the activity is completed. Cleaning up after each work period necessitates leaving the environment clean. Individual as well as committee endeavours may be planned with teacher guidance. Developing of standards and assessment in terms of these criteria helps pupils stay on track and persevere. Quality oral communication is inherent in the project method of instruction.

Problem solving experiences aid pupils in perceiving the need to communicate effectively with others. A relevant problem in an ongoing lesson/unit of study may be identified. The problem is salient and must be clear in meaning for participants. Seeking information from a variety of reference sources including knowledgeable resource personnel, the internet and the world wide web, might well bring much content to bear for discussion in attempting to solve the problem. An hypothesis needs to be developed which needs testing in a lifelike experience. The hypothesis might then be accepted as is, modified, or refuted (See Parker, 2001).

Project methods as well as problem solving activities emphasize heavy pupil involvement in sequencing leanings from beginning of each to the end. The teacher serves as a resource person and assists learners to stay on task toward completion of the project as well as the problem solving experience. Oral communication skills are greatly needed in any group endeavour, be it small or large group settings. It is a basic in the curriculum and applicable to all curriculum areas. In social studies, in particular, each inherent academic discipline requires clarity in speaking and quality listening behaviours. Among committee members, the flow of the discussion should circulate within the group. All need be to participate actively with no one dominating the discussion.

Thus, in the following examples, pertaining to oral communication, it is salient to communicate clearly in each academic discipline:

- history in planning a time line to show sequence of events
- geography when developing a relief map of the geographical region being studied
- economics involving the making of a chart showing goods and services in dollar amounts, produced, within selected nations in the ongoing lesson/unit of study
- political science in planning cooperatively showing lines of organization in government. This could relate to the federal level (legislative, executive, and judicial), the state level, as well as the city government level
- sociology/anthropology with culture being integrated into the social studies. Society and how it affects people in every day affairs is the focal point of discussion. The Old Order Amish, for example, provide subject matter for a study of culture. They dress in unique ways which differentiate from members in the larger society. Women and girls wear prayer caps and long dresses which extend to the ankles and the wrists. The dresses, with high neck lines, are always of a plain colour such as blue, purple, black, never striped or checked. The men and boys wear blue denim trousers and single coloured shirts for weekday work duties. Straw hats are worn in summer. Worship services are conducted in German, bi-weekly in homes as well as in barns in spring and summer (See Medina and Costa, 2010).

A sample of learning activities for each of the above named academic disciplines involving subject matter for the social studies is given. These need expanding so that pupils may understand and attach meaning to what is being studied. People must be studied from diverse academic disciplines. They possess an historical background within a geographical region, buying goods and services, and are governed by federal, state, and local levels. Culture influences behaviour within society. Society then has its values, customs, and beliefs which it inculcates in the societal arenas. The influence of culture may be seen most strongly in primary groups such as The Old Order Amish, as well as the Hutterite Mennonites, a communal society, in South Dakota, North Dakota, Montana, Washington state, and in Canada.

Social Action in the Curriculum

There are improvements which need to be made in society. Advocating actively that these need to be made stresses social action.

Recommendations must be made based on evidence, not shallow thinking. Pupils may choose a learning station in the classroom titled Social Action. There are possible tasks for pupils to work on which they perceive as being poignant. The ideal is that these come from learners with teacher guidance. There are problems such as the following which exist in school/society:

- stop signs needed at selected intersections due to heavy traffic. Stop lights might well be necessary in some of these places
- a polluted stream or creek located near to the local school
- litter on the school grounds which learners may take pride in eliminating so that an attractive school ground may come about
- odours in the school bathrooms
- unattractive classrooms. Perhaps some easy to do items can improve the situation such as bulletin boards, neatly displayed library books, and putting all waste paper in the trash container.

Increasingly, more salient items may be tackled with a social action approach in the curriculum. The major goal and objective in the social studies is to develop good citizens. Certainly quality social action programmes may make their contributions to societal improvement (Ediger, 2007).

REFERENCES

Ediger, Marlow (2010), "Constructivism and the Social Studies," *Edutracks*, 9 (7), 13-14.

Ediger, Marlow (2007), "Learning Activities in the Curriculum," *College Student Journal*, 41 (4), 967-969.

Guilfoyle, Christy (2006), "Is There Life Beyond NCLB?" *Educational Leadership*, 64 (3),8-13.

Medina, Carmen L., and Maria del Rocio Costa (2010), "Collaborative Voices Exploring Culturally and Socially Responsive Literacies," *Language Arts*, 87 (4), 263-276.

National Council for the Social Studies (1997), Curri*culum Standards for the Social Studies.* Edison, New York: Whitehurst and Clark.

Parker, Walter C. (2001), *Social Studies in Elementary Education.* Upper Saddle River, New Jersey: Merrill, Prentice Hall.

27

Literature in the Social Studies

The Pupil and the Teacher

Pupils need to experience the kinds of literature in the social studies, as it relates to the ongoing unit of study. This is necessary in order that individual differences are provided in the classroom. Learners differ from each other in interests, purposes and abilities in reading. Background information for achievement in the ensuing unit must be possessed by each pupil so that the new learnings can be understood. Reading social studies subject matters should teach lessons to the pupils so that it is beneficial for them across the curriculum. Thus, useful content and skills in reading transfer to other subject matter areas. Reading is an important skill to emphasize in the curriculum.

Developing Abilities in Reading Social Studies Content

Ausubel (1958) stressed the saliency of pupils possessing background reading to benefit from the new content to be taught. Thus, he advocated the use of advanced organizers. Directly related to the ensuing literary content, the advance organizer provided brief background information to prepare learners for comprehending new subject matter. This would sequence new subject matter with the old and improve pupil's understanding of major facts, concepts, and generalizations. Ausubel believed that pupils having sufficient background information before pursuing new knowledge, was a fact factor in learning. A seamless preparation to understand the ensuing is necessary and makes for quality teaching. *Secondly*, learners must attach meaning to ongoing reading experiences. Literature becomes meaningless unless it possesses depth and breadth of understanding. A major problem in reading might relate to vocabulary difficulties. If pupils do not attach meaning to vocabulary contained in the reading selection, they might be turned off from the selection being read. Here, the literature teacher has all the responsibilities of assisting pupils in vocabulary development. Thus, in silent reading, unknown words may be pronounced incorrectly unless the learner raises his/her hand for assistance. As the pupil continues silent reading, clarity of word meaning may not be fulfilled. The learner may also ask the teacher for word meanings in silent reading as the need arises. Fluency in reading is salient! The glossary and appropriate grade level dictionary are additional resources (See Tichman, 2008).

Third, when using the basic textbook, the teacher may print the words neatly for all to see on the chalkboard/white board. The teacher points to each word as it is being pronounced clearly and correctly. The word should also be used in a meaningful sentence. This total procedure might as well provide background information for reading. A purpose may be identified in terms of questions, printed on the chalk/white board, to answer in the ensuing reading activity. Pupils as well as the teacher need to choose these questions. As a follow-up experience, pupils should discuss these questions in the classroom. Here, critical and creative reading, as well as problem solving might be emphasized. Pupil comprehension must be stressed.

Fourth, pupils may need assistance in word recognition. There can be different ways used here, such as pronouncing the word immediately when a learner raises his/her hand at the time of reading and asking for help. Context clues too is a good procedure, where a pupil who hesitates on an unknown word is asked to give one which makes sense in relationship to the rest of the words in the sentence. If this is not quete enough, the respected pupil needs to look at the beginning letter, also, generally a consonant, to sound out the word. Sounding out words may be used to identify unknown words as the need arises as well as when sound/symbol relationships are consistent. Phonics is merely a tool to identify unknown words in reading; making sense of sentences in reading comprehension is necessary and not phonic learning for its own sake (Ediger and Rao, 2011).

Fifth, pupil's choice of interesting reading materials for sustained silent reading becomes highly important. Interest propels effort for reading and learning. There should be a time allotted in the daily schedule for learners in reading self selected materials. Generally, materials chosen for reading are on the comprehension level of the pupil. The teacher may suggest materials if the learner cannot settle down with a reading activity. The writer when supervising university teachers in the public schools has observed pupil success in reading when they chose what to read in sustained silent reading. Usually, all in a classroom are involved in reading to themselves with self selected materials. Periodically, the teacher calls pupils to a designated area in the classroom for a quiet conference which does not disturb other readers. Questions were asked of learners pertaining to content read to evaluate comprehension as well as having the pupil read a brief passage orally to assess fluency in reading (Ediger, 2011).

Sixth, the attitudinal dimension toward reading should be evaluated. An inward desire to read must be in the offing. Goleman (1996) emphasizes the importance of Emotional Intelligence whereby the attitudes of pupils can be as salient as as knowledge and skills. Negative attitudes hinder learner progress in school and later at the work place. Learners need to be guided to enjoy the different academic disciplines and thus possess favourable feelings toward each curriculum area.

The attitudinal dimension is equally relevant in developing good human relationships in the classroom. Rudeness, put downs, talking back, and criticizing are negative behaviours and disrupt achievement. Rather, rules of conduct need to be posted in the classroom and systematically reviewed with pupils to notice progress or lack thereof in these vital areas of the attitudinal dimension.

Seventh, self efficacy (Bandura 1997) is an important concept to stress in teaching and learning situations. Self efficacy indicates that the social studies teacher develops confidence in the self to become a master. Through reflexion, inservice education, conferences with other professionals, as well as doing considerable professional reading, the teacher becomes a devout, competent instructor who is able to work well with pupils of different cultures, abilities, and talents. He/she is able to provide for individual differences in assisting each learner to achieve more optimally. The ability to plan quality objectives, learning opportunities to attain the objectives, as well as evaluation procedures which are valid and reliable to ascertain learner progress. Literature of diverse genres in ongoing social studies units of study should assist pupils to do well.

REFERENCES

Ausubel, David (1958), *The Psychology of Meaningful Verbal Learning.* New York: Grune and Stratton.

Bandura, Albert (1997), *Self Efficacy: The Exercise of Control.* New York: Freeman.

Ediger, Marlow (2011), "Shared Reading, The Pupil, and the Teacher," *Reading Improvement*, 48 (2), 55-58.

Ediger, Marlow, and D. Bhaskara Rao (2011), *Essays in Teaching Reading.* New Delhi, India; Discovery Publishing House.

Goleman, Daniel (,1995), *Emotional Intelligence*. New York: Bantam Books,

Tichman, Barbara (2008),"The Object of Their Attention," *Educational Leadership*, 65 (5), 44-47.

Index

A

B

C